the Diana Look

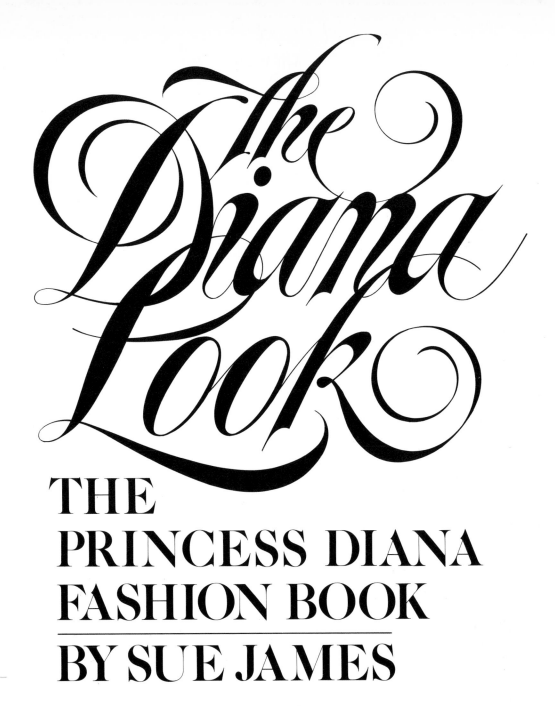

the Diana Look

THE PRINCESS DIANA FASHION BOOK

BY SUE JAMES

Photographs
TIM GRAHAM

Fashion drawings
LESLEY DILCOCK

William Morrow and Company, Inc.
New York 1984

Back cover photograph: Rex Features, London

Frontispiece, facing page 3; white cotton jacquard dress by Benny Ong, Ayers Rock 1983. Page 7; cream coloured organza and lace trim evening gown by Gina Fratini, Auckland 1983. Page 127; with Prince William at Kensington Palace 1982, dress by the Chelsea Design Company.

Planned and produced by Robert MacDonald Publishing
Designed by Bridget Morley and Sue Rawkins
© Robert MacDonald Publishing, Sue James 1984
Previously published in Great Britain by
Orbis Publishing Limited
London 1984

Library of Congress Catalog Card Number – 83–63077

ISBN: 0–688–03163–3
ISBN: 0–688–03172–2 (pbk)

Typeset by Ace Filmsetting, Frome
Originated and printed by Mateu Cromo Artes Graficas S.A. Spain

First U.S. Edition
1 2 3 4 5 6 7 8 9 10

Contents

Preface

I have thoroughly enjoyed writing this book. It has been a pleasure from beginning to end—or very nearly so. I doubt if there are many authors who could say the same.

Foremost among the reasons for this must be the subject of the book, the Princess of Wales, herself. If, as I have done, you spend many hours analysing her outfits, looking at hundreds or thousands of photographs, and talking at first hand to many of her favourite designers, it is difficult to end up without a feeling of enormous respect for Princess Diana, both for her sheer stylishness, and for her personality generally. She has achieved a remarkable transformation, from teenage girl to elegant woman, an undoubted Queen in the making, in a remarkably short space of time. Her influence on our attitudes to Royalty and on fashion as a whole has been undeniable and considerable.

One of the things that has most increased my admiration for the Princess is the respect in which she is held by the designers of her clothes. It is sometimes thought that Diana has it all done for her; that there are experts and advisers on hand to tell her what to wear and when and how to wear it. This turns out to be far from the truth. Diana is a young lady with her own very definite taste, and with very positive views about clothes. One after another, her designers have confirmed that working on her clothes is not just a privilege but a pleasure.

To the designers themselves, I owe an enormous debt of gratitude. They have contributed original design sketches to the book, and have given me their time with great generosity. Special mention must be made of Donald Campbell, Gina Fratini, Bruce Oldfield, Jan Vanvelden, Belinda Belville and David Sassoon of Belville Sassoon, Victor Edelstein, Arabella Pollen, Julie Fortescue and David Bates of David Neil, Benny Ong and Jo Osborne and Sally Muir of Warm and Wonderful, all of whom have allowed us to use designer's drawings of clothes that have been worn by the Princess. The drawings all say something of the skill that goes into sophisticated dress design. I also owe my profoundest thanks to Barbara Daly, our top make-up authority, for explaining some of her professional methods, and to John Boyd, Royal milliner, for sparing me his time to talk about hats. Their contributions have been of great value to me.

Janice Collier, top beauty journalist and friend, wrote the sections on health and beauty far better than I could have done. And Lesley Dilcock has interpreted my suggestions for fashion drawings with enormous skill. Tim Graham's expertise as a photographer is evident on almost every page of the book: I owe him my thanks for illustrating so well virtually everything I wanted to say—and more besides. I also want to thank my secretary, Kim, for spending so many hours deciphering my notes, and finally, my husband and daughter for their immense patience.

As I have said, writing this book was a pleasure. I have also learned from it. The Princess of Wales was given a great opportunity to set an example of stylish dressing and, where other women might have let it go by, she seized it with enthusiasm. We can all benefit from this example; that is what this book is about. If it helps any woman who reads it to dress with more confidence, awareness and style, it will have achieved what it set out to do.

Sue James   October 1983

CHAPTER ONE

The Essence of Style

From the moment Lady Diana Spencer stepped out at her first public engagement wearing a strapless black silk taffeta evening dress, we were all captivated. The occasion was a recital to raise money for a new extension to the Royal Opera House at Goldsmiths Hall London in March 1981, and the dress was designed by David and Elizabeth Emanuel. This lady we told ourselves is not only a Princess to be; she has *style*. It was a spectacular debut.

Since then, Lady Diana Spencer, now the Princess of Wales, has become one of the leading ladies of fashion. It was always inevitable that marriage to the heir to the throne would turn the spotlight of public attention on her, but it was certainly not inevitable that she would join the ranks of the 'superstars', becoming one of the most photographed and talked about people in the world. Her wardrobe, hairstyles and make-up are scrutinised by fascinated women from all walks of life. Designers who, a few years ago, were known only to a select group of fashion conscious women, have become internationally famous for dressing the Princess of Wales. She could have achieved none of this had she been no more than a Princess, but she is not. She is a Princess with *style*.

Style is what this book is all about. It is a quality that is undefinable, something that no amount of money can buy. If you give three women the same dress to wear, the one who stands out will be the one who wears it with style. It may be no more than the way she ties her scarf, or the belt she chooses, but whatever it is, she looks different. Having style means dressing distinctively, in a way that is entirely your own. Style is always personal; what works for one person is quite wrong for another. And it definitely cannot be bought; you don't acquire style just by buying expensive clothes. Some women can look far more stunning in an off-the-peg chain store outfit than other women in designer's outfits costing three times as much. The Princess of Wales is one of them.

If you are aware of your clothes and the way you look, you can learn to dress with style. Princess Diana has natural style. She doesn't just wear good clothes; she has the knack of knowing what looks best and when and how to wear it. Like most women, she has made a few mistakes, especially at the beginning when she was finding her style, but she has learned by them. She also knows that being stylish does not mean being a fashion follower, nor an innovator, and because of this she is undoubtedly our most successful fashion ambassador.

Unlike most women, the Princess of Wales has had to cope with the need to change her whole style of dress. In 1981, although it now seems much longer ago than that, she was sharing a South Kensington flat with friends and teaching in a Kensington kindergarten. Her favourite clothes were casuals—a cashmere sweater and floral skirt or jeans and a t-shirt. Her engagement to the Prince of Wales meant a complete change of lifestyle. From that moment on she became a public figure, eternally subjected to the scrutiny of the press and called on to carry out one of the most difficult jobs imaginable, that of the future Queen of England. For a young girl, it must have seemed awesomely difficult. But Lady Diana proved herself more than equal to the task.

Imitation is the sincerest form of flattery, and no other measure of the Princess's success is needed than the number of women from all over the world who have copied her style of dress. Clothes in 'Ladi Di' styles and colours have invaded the high street stores, and dressmakers the world over have found themselves

Below; Lady Diana Spencer, as the world first saw her, and an example of the simple separates she preferred for her work in a Kensington nursery school. Facing page; the famous black silk taffeta evening gown, designed by David and Elizabeth Emanuel, in which Lady Diana caught the public's attention in no uncertain way, and signalled her intention of breaking away from the old Royal fashion style.

Left; the Princess's love of bright colours was apparent at an early stage, as demonstrated by the Jasper Conran red silk suit she wore in Tetbury in Gloucestershire in 1981. Above; the pale pastel suit Diana wore at Ascot in the summer of 1981, is a good example of the Princess's versatility in her use of her wardrobe. The dress was worn again without the blouse on honeymoon, and the blouse itself has appeared with several different outfits. Facing page; an off-the-peg suit from Jaeger for the last day of the Welsh tour in Brecon in the autumn of 1981. The matching hat was in a style that was to become one of her distinctive trademarks.

copying minute details of sleeves, collars and cuffs. There must be millions of women who have one of the famous romantic frilled blouses in their wardrobes, a reminder of June 1981, when marriage was in the air and romance and feminity had blossomed into fashion.

The Princess-to-be signalled her taste for pretty, distinctive clothes from the very beginning. The colourful red silk suit and characteristic 'Lady Di' blouse, which she wore to meet neighbours in Tetbury, Gloucestershire, and the soft pastel suit which she wore to Ascot in the summer of 1981, are just two examples. The rest of the fashion world followed close on her heels. Frills, ruffles, demure details that weren't too fussy, became the focal points of collars, blouses and dresses. The famous pearl choker, worn both for day and evening, also had its effect. Pearls came back into vogue and were worn by women of all ages. Even the sapphire and diamond engagement ring, when it was duly revealed to the public, was copied and was soon on sale at every price throughout the range. Lady Diana chose sapphire blue for the official engagement photographs too, wearing a suit by Cojana from Harrods. Above all, Lady Diana brought hats back into popular fashion. From pretty pill-box or tiny feathered tricorn-shapes, to high brimmed hats and floppy berets (most of them designed by milliner John Boyd), Diana wore them all. She showed that frills and feathers, carefully chosen, need not look out of place however smart and formal the occasion.

If the Royal romance and wedding was a fairy story come true, then it was in her evening wear that Diana seemed most like a fairy tale Princess. It was here that she first began to excel, and here that she was at her most dazzling. From delicate chiffons to shimmering taffetas, her ballgowns have never failed to raise approving comments. The marvellous ballgown she wore to the Splendour of the Gonzago exhibition at the Victoria and Albert Museum in November 1981 shows Diana at her most bewitching and demure; designed by Belville Sassoon, it was made in beautiful silk chiffon in delicate pastel shades (see p 93 for the original design of this dress). Not surprisingly, ballgowns and long dresses were soon being worn by both young and old for formal evening wear. Her off-the-shoulder bodices have remained firm favourites, but the Princess has also kept her ability to surprise us all. The stunning one-shoulder cream and silver beaded ballgown she wore at the Melbourne Hilton in Australia in April 1983 (and later to the premiere of *Octopussy* in London) was the perfect answer to those Australian critics who had suggested that her style of dress had become too conventional. This body skimming dress, with its elegance and regal sex-appeal, emphasises the

The fairy-tale Princess; Diana's evening wear has consistently delighted and amazed. Below left; bewitching and demure in an off-the-shoulder silk chiffon ballgown by Belville Sassoon, at the Splendour of the Gonzago exhibition in November 1981. Below right; one of her most memorable evening dresses was this slinky one-shoulder design by Hachi, worn in Australia in April 1983 and again at the premier of Octopussy *in London.*

extent to which the Princess has brought back the meaning of glamour to evening dress.

The essentials of Lady Diana's style were all apparent at an early stage, in particular her love of bright, vivid colours. She soon replaced the dark, rather dull, colours we used to see worn for formal occasions with eye-catching reds, blues and pinks, and then followed these colour themes through in her accessories. Conventional blacks and browns were banished, especially for shoes, in favour of cheerful colours that matched her outfits. A perfect example was the sophisticated but simple two-piece in red and blue silk crêpe-de-chine, designed by David Neil, which she wore to Nicholas Soames' wedding in May 1981. Worn with a soft frilled neckline, side button top and an easy wrapover skirt, the outfit was very striking. The 'two-piece' suit style was also an early favourite. Almost too casual to be called 'smart' the style was quickly adopted by the fashion pundits. The cropped jacket with velvet trim and matching full circular skirt—which proved so appropriate for her visit to the staff of Capital Radio—was a style she wore several times; it topped the fashion charts in the winter of 1982.

Below left; the colourful two-piece suit in red and blue silk crêpe-de-chine, designed by David Neil, was another early indication of Diana's taste for strong colours. First seen at Nicholas Soames' wedding in May 1981, it reappeared during the Australian tour two years later. Below right; the Chelsea Design Company's two-piece suit, worn for a visit to Capital Radio, was very much a fashion statement for the times.

The essentials of the Princess's style changed hardly at all during pregnancy. The brightly coloured fringed coat by Belville Sassoon and the veiled blue hat by John Boyd, with matching accessories, seen at the Guildhall in London, were entirely in character.

By Christmas 1981, the world knew that the Princess of Wales was expecting a baby. How would she reconcile the demands of her public image with her pregnancy? In the event, with her flair and her contemporary outlook, she easily kept her stylish looks. And her influence on maternity wear turned out to be as fresh and beneficial as it had been in other areas. Her simply cut dresses with all the 'Diana' details – soft frilled necklines, simple sailor collars in soft wools and silks – were just right. In fact, she retained a style that was very similar to that of her non-maternity outfits. The colourful Belville Sassoon coat with fringed detail, topped with a veiled hat, which she wore to the Guildhall in London, was only one of her striking outfits during this time.

The Royal tours of 1983 completed the transformation of the Princess into a slim, elegant and confident lady of fashion. Right; a cool-coloured silk dress, in the style of the Chelsea Design Company, for a visit to St John's, New Brunswick. From the drop-waist to the double-breasted bodice and the neckline frill, the Princess has interpreted every point of fashion. Far right; a very tailored look in this Jasper Conran suit, worn in Canada and on several other occasions. The collarless neckline, fly-front jacket and straight-cut skirt show the Princess's taste for simplicity.

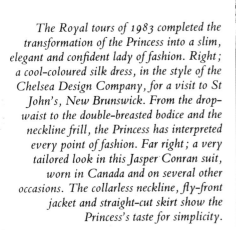

The Princess of Wales had little time to relax after the birth of her first child. Within a very short time, she was back at the centre of the public stage, looking, if possible, more elegant and more beautiful than ever before. And nowhere was she seen to better effect than on the Royal tours of Australia, New Zealand and Canada in 1983. By this time, the Princess's role as a leader of fashion was known throughout the world, and millions of women waited with happy anticipation to see what she would wear. The Princess did not disappoint them. She took with her a splendid wardrobe, containing some old favourites and some new ideas, but demonstrating as always her ability to adapt modern fashion to suit her own individual style. Pastels remained a favourite choice, as in the cool-coloured drop-waist dress, in the style of the Chelsea Design Company, that she wore in St John's, New Brunswick. The soft frilled neckline she wore with it has remained one of her trade-marks in dressing. A newer look was the simple, very fashionable and distinctive printed silk suit by Jan Vanvelden, with its kimono-shaped jacket, full soft skirt and winged-collar blouse. (See page 68.) It shows just how Diana incorporates fashion trends into her own style of dressing—by picking a fashion style point and using it in an unobvious way to achieve an understated way of looking smart. Her tailored cream suit by Jasper Conran, with collarless neckline, fly-front jacket and straight-cut skirt shows the value of understated smartness. This outfit was elegant precisely because it was so simple. It was also smart because it was worn with confidence. Throughout the tours, the Princess looked poised, confident and relaxed, despite the continuous presence of press photographers and television cameras, and however formal the occasion. The Princess has learned to have confidence in her clothes, and confidence in your clothes always shines through. She has also proved that these 'special occasion' clothes, which British designers do so well, can look chic and relaxed in almost any circumstances.

The Princess has the knack of wearing the right clothes on the right occasions. She understands the essence of style. You can argue that it is easy to look good if you have plenty of nice clothes or if you have the face or figure to go with more or less anything. But it takes much more than that—a lot of time and a lot of effort—to develop a sense of occasion, to pick clothes that are appropriate, and to wear them with style. The Princess may appear to do this with ease, but appearances can be deceptive. Such effects are not achieved without great care and without attention to the basic principles of good dress sense. We can see what these principles are by looking at what the Princess herself wears, and what her outfits have in common. The main points, then, are these: simplicity; practicality and suitability; and sense of colour. The Princess demonstrates them all.

Simplicity in style does not mean playing safe and being boring. It means letting your clothes speak for you in a very 'simple' way. Always remember that clothes reflect your personality, so what you choose to wear is very personal. The key to this is to aim for an 'understated' style—in other words to go for clothes that are not fussy or extravagant in shape, colour or style. For example, the Princess sometimes wears a blouse with a frilled neckline, but she never overdoes the effect by wearing a skirt with a frill around the hem, which would destroy the simple touch of femininity. This is what 'understated' means.

Simplicity does not mean being predictable. Try putting together the not-so-obvious. Take, for example, a smart blazer suit: don't always wear it with a basic collared shirt but soften it with a frilled or bow-necked blouse, or even a simple t-shirt. But, as with dresses, stick to a single detail—a frill, a pleat or a ruffle, but not all three. Princess Diana knows this rule of simplicity well. The coat dress in grey wool flannel with velvet trim, which she wore to launch a ship in Liverpool, was totally uncluttered and definitely very chic.

Above; a grey wool flannel coat dress, designed by Arabella Pollen, which the Princess wore to launch a ship in Liverpool. The classic colours were surprisingly unobtrusive for a Royal event, but the uncluttered style made the dress stand out with ease. Facing page; the Princess demonstrates her unerring sense of occasion in this simple black dress by Jasper Conran at the funeral of Princess Grace of Monaco—an occasion about which the Princess obviously felt very deeply.

Practicability and suitability go hand in hand. Practicality is really a matter of common sense; it means thinking ahead to where you are going to be and what you will be doing. You don't wear a pair of elegant pumps if you are going to be standing in a muddy field for the afternoon. Nor, probably, will you want to wear a low-cut dress if you are going to spend a lot of time bending over. This is something that the Princess has to bear in mind all the time. With photographers eager to pounce on her slightest slip (or lack of it) she cannot afford to forget the practical aspects of her appearance. Suitability is the other side of the coin. Diana can no more wear something unsuitable than she can wear something impractical. With her continual round of state visits and official functions, Diana obviously has more need to consider practicality and suitability than most of us, but all of us attend special occasions at some time or another and, like the Princess, need to dress correctly.

In other words, we need to develop a sense of occasion—of what is suitable and what unsuitable. Different occasions demand different approaches. The Princess of Wales knows this and would never allow fashion to rule over her good sense. For the funeral of Princess Grace of Monaco in September 1982, she wore a simple black dress designed by Jasper Conran that was neither drab nor too dramatic, cool and comfortable because it was in silk, and very suitable and practical for such an important state occasion.

Two examples of the Princess's stylish use of colour. Above left; variations on a single colour, in this ice-cool pink outfit designed by the Chelsea Design Company and worn at a state barbecue. Above right; a combination of two contrasting colours, green and bright red (incidentally the Welsh colours), in Donald Campbell's design for a visit to Caernarvon Castle in 1981.

Colours play a major part in dressing smartly. You need to choose colours that not only look good themselves but which make you feel comfortable. An easy guideline to follow is to be positive—whether you are stepping out in scarlet or mixing soft blues and greys. Princess Diana's style is a perfect example of colour coordination. She has strong positive views about colours—they are either striking and vibrant or soft and pastel—and she builds on a single colour theme whether the occasion is formal or informal. Pink is one of her favourite colours, as in the ice-cool pink outfit designed by the Chelsea Design Company for a state barbecue. You can see how she has followed the colours through in her accessories too.

If the Princess is not dressed entirely in one colour, she will often cleverly mix two colours together. Sometimes they are just tones apart, but at other times they are contrasting, as in the outfit designed by Donald Campbell for her trip to Caernarvon Castle in Wales in 1981. The green skirt and blouse made an effective contrast to the bright red hat, jacket, shoes and bag (and also managed to combine the Welsh colours). This is a useful technique since it enables a favourite colour to be worn further away from the face, should it clash with hair colouring for example. Gone are the old rules that you buy hat and shoes to match. Coordination has become the name of the game—and for fabrics just as much as for colours. Mixed plain and patterned, providing that it is done correctly, can have the most eye-catching effect. (See p 24 for fabric coordination).

Colours need to work for you and not against you. Not all colours will suit your complexion or hair colour. How disastrous it could be to dress from head to toe in bright red if it clashed violently with your cheek colouring, or perhaps with your carrot-coloured hair. Getting the colours right in the first place is half the battle. As a general guide, if you are very pale and fair opt for strong positive colours that put colour into your looks. If you are very dark, avoid dark muddy browns, olives or black, as they can drown your looks. The Princess of Wales uses colour cleverly. She is fully aware of the colours that suit her hair and skin tones and avoids the ones that don't. Once again, she provides an ideal example for us all to follow.

Finally, walk and wear your clothes with confidence; they always look so much better. Many women lack confidence, especially when it comes to choosing and wearing more formal clothes. Have the confidence to follow your own taste and to wear clothes you feel happy in. Even if everyone tells you that you look marvellous in a certain style, don't wear it if you don't feel happy in it. And never buy clothes that are too tight. A smaller size label inside a dress may persuade you that you are thinner than you really are, but the truth is that you would have looked slimmer and more attractive in a larger size. Have confidence in the colours you choose. If you have decided to wear a red dress, shoes, bag and hat, don't cover the whole outfit up with a heavy dark overcoat, or destroy the colour scheme by introducing a lot of other colours. Confidence is, in some ways, the last ingredient of dressing well. Even when you have everything else right, you still need confidence in yourself, your looks and your clothes to be really stylish.

The Princess of Wales has obviously learned all the essentials of dressing well, and now maintains an amazingly high standard. For her, however, things have become, in some ways, more rather than less difficult. Gone are the days when she could nip into one of her favourite high street stores—Harrods, Harvey Nichols, Laura Ashley or Benetton. The watchful presence of a phalanx of security guards makes casual shopping impossible. She now has to get other people to shop for her. Fashion experts from *Vogue* often help by putting together a selection of clothes for her to choose from. And although she is in touch with many top designers, she certainly doesn't have all her clothes designed for her. 'One of the greatest compliments I have been paid,' says top designer Gina Fratini, 'is that the Princess has chosen clothes from my collection.' In other words, she often goes for off-the-peg designs that are readily available in the shops. 'Occasionally she will ask for a slight alteration,' explains Gina, 'but not always.'

Diana knows what she likes and has very positive views. Her interest in clothes is refreshing but by no means obsessive. 'She's wonderful to work with because she is interested in what you are doing,' says Jan Vanvelden, one of her designers. Certainly it is to the delight of all our designers that someone like the Princess of Wales dresses so well and looks so good, and, seemingly always (apart from a few odd accessories), wears British. One thing is certain; it can't be failed to be recognised that Princess Diana has put British fashion back firmly on the map, right where it belongs.

Building up a basic wardrobe

Any woman with style will tend to buy investment clothes, at least for the mainstays in her wardrobe. A coat, suit, classic skirts, shirts and pants, and smart dresses can be an expensive outlay, but they are all clothes that can go on from season to season and from year to year. To make such items a worthwhile investment however, you need to get mileage from your clothes. Impulse buys are something that no busy woman can either afford or have time for. Shopping for clothes can be a chore, however much you may enjoy it, so you need to decide what you want before you go out to look for it. Mistakes are always made when you panic and buy the wrong thing.

Concentrating on your basic wardrobe doesn't have to limit your looks. Most high street shops these days sell clothes that come in a range of styles which all work together, so that you can swap them around and wear them in many different ways. For obvious reasons, this mainly applies to separates, although some simple dresses can be more versatile. A linen wrap style dress, for example, can also be worn as a lightweight coat, or a simply shaped shift dress can be belted and teamed with a skirt to give a tunic effect. Coordination may not be the height of 'street fashion' these days, but for the woman who wants to dress stylishly and a little more individually, dress coordination, using carefully chosen colours and fabrics that work well together, can be the answer.

Here are the basic guidelines to follow when planning your investments.
1. Always buy clothes because they suit you and not because they are in fashion.
2. Choosing the right colours is of prime importance. Work out a colour scheme, just as you would before painting a room. Buying the wrong colour garment can be a costly mistake. Look at what you already have and decide which colours are prominent in your wardrobe. If they are browns, creams and blacks, then it would be unwise to rush out and buy a navy suit. Don't buy lots of printed clothes—classic printed dresses date much more quickly than plain ones, and you will tire of wearing them too. The best principle is to stick to the neutral colours for expensive items, such as coats, suits, trouser suits, classic dresses, and skirts, and then to introduce new fashion colours with accessories and smaller items like blouses, sweaters, t-shirts and so on. The chart on p 23 will give you some ideas.
3. Once you have decided on a basic colour scheme, then buy your classics in these colours. Good classic or investment buys are often worth investigating at sale time. A cashmere coat down to half price has to be a good bargain. Watch out for top brand names or specialised designer shops with discounted prices. You may easily find a classic coat, dress or skirt with the extra fashion detail to make it rather special.
4. Liven up your investment buys with colourful t-shirts, tops, blouses and sweaters in a recommended highlighting colour.
5. Finally, choose your accessories carefully. The wrong one can turn an expensive outfit into a disaster. Decide on your basic list of essential accessories—a good court shoe, low-heeled pumps, two or three leather belts, a silk scarf and a wool shawl would be a good starting point.

On the next three pages are more detailed suggestions as to how to go about choosing the main items and on how to combine them to create a really stylish, and lasting wardrobe.

The basic wardrobe

Coats. A good winter coat can cost a fortune, unless you find a bargain in the sales. But you will need one. Stick to classic styles, like a double breasted overcoat, a simple wrap and tie or a classic redincote. Never buy a coat that is too short since you will have to wear it over many different lengths. A good choice is about two inches below the knee. Raincoats, too, should be in a fairly traditional style, for example a trench coat. It doesn't have to be too expensive; there are plenty of cheaper ones available.

Jackets. Decide which you are likely to wear the most – a smart blazer style or a casual one. If you can afford both, so much the better. The blazer will look good for smart occasions with skirts, dresses and pants. The bigger casual jacket will go with cords, denims and more informal separates. Choose the one that best suits your lifestyle.

Dresses. Pick a classic style which will carry on for a few seasons; a plain shirtwaister, an easy wrap dress or a coat dress that can look both smart or casual. If you keep them simple, you can dress them up with each new season's fashion accessories.

Skirts. Choose one that suits your shape. Do you look slimmer in a straight cut skirt? Or are pleats your favourites? Or maybe a soft dirndl. Ideally, you should have one of each, either full or straight, in heavy and lightweight fabrics. You can buy them gradually over a period of time. A tweed skirt goes well with sweaters and shirts. And a straight gaberdine skirt looks good for daytime with shirts or t-shirts, and for the evening with a dressy blouse or top.

Shirts and blouses. Try and build up a selection of styles, from high-neck soft blouses to men's style shirts. It is worth considering a blouse with a detachable cravat or tie, so that you can wear it in different ways. Or buy two or three similar styles that you know suit you, but have them in different fabrics.

Sweaters. Classics all the way – lambswool, Angora, shetland and cashmeres with simple v-necks, round or roll necks. Never buy them too small; a bigger fitting sweater looks much more stylish. Slipovers and waistcoats, either plain or patterned, like a fairisle, are

silk blouse

wrap coat

classic sweater

tweed skirt

leather boots

ideal because of their versatility. Wear them with a blouse, a finer sweater or even with a dress. They can act as another, warmer, layer in the winter, or as a lightweight top in summer.

Trousers. A well-cut pair of pleated-front pants, with a straight cut leg that isn't too narrow, always looks good. Your other pair, of course, must be denims or cords. Always go for plain trousers; nothing in a textured or patterned fabric. Navy, grey, black, soft fawn and burgundy are good classic colours for trousers.

Footwear. You should have, at the very least, a pair of court shoes, a simple flat pump, low heeled sandals and a good pair of boots. But, as we all know, no sooner have you worn out one pair of shoes than the others all seem to follow.

You should really have two pairs of
shoes on the go all the time; one in a
conventional dark colour, one brighter
pair that have a more fashionable feel.
For summer, have a comfortable pair of
sandals that are still stylish, and, for
winter, have a good classic pair of boots
– brown, black or grey are again the
best colours. Leather is a much better
buy than cheaper alternatives. However,
suede and some fabrics like grosgrain are
ideal for the summer and for evenings.
You can find plenty of reasonable
imitations, but do watch out as they tend
to make your feet very hot. Canvas,
rubber and some fun plastics are good
for summer sandals and casuals, but
bear in mind that they won't last.

Scarves. These are relatively cheap. But
it is still worth looking out for bargains
in silk and wool, especially around sale
time. Try and build up a stock of good
strong colours in various sizes – long,
square, shawl, kerchief etc.

Belts. It is worth investing in several
belts; a wide soft leather style, a narrow
one and a 'trouser' belt. The heavier
weight belts are often cheaper in men's
shops. Double up on belts by using long
scarves worn around the waist as
cummerbunds.

Jewellery. We would all love to wear
the real thing. But if that isn't possible,
then good modern fake costume
jewellery can work just as well, and
sometimes even better. Jewellery is
discussed in detail in later chapters, but
one golden rule is worth mentioning
here: never overdo it. You will look
much better with a single bold piece
than with an assortment of different
chains, bracelets, earrings and necklaces
that don't match.

Tights. The range of leg colours and
patterns that tights are available in is
enormous. Ringing the changes in the
colour or pattern of your tights is an
excellent way of giving a new chic look
to an old dress or skirt. Try harmonising
the colour of your tights with the other
shades you are wearing. A navy skirt can
look very elegant with navy tights and
shoes. A tartan dress can look young and
fun if you pick out a dominant colour
like bright red and follow it through in
your leg colour. In general, dark
coloured tights don't look at all stylish
with light coloured strappy sandals.
They can, however, be very effective

...linen jacket...

...patterned shawl...

...clutch bag...

...shirt-waister dress...

...bright scarf...

...casual blouson...

...flecked sweater...

...leather satchel...

...corduroy trousers...

...patterned socks...

...flat shoes...

Basic colours	Highlighting colours
Black, grey and white	Red, electric blue, yellow, pink and cream
Navy, white and red	Softer shades of blue, black, grey and strong vibrant greens
Browns and creams	Ginger, terracotta, black, mustard and scarlet
Plum and burgundy	Grey, cream, fuschia pink, electric blue and mustard
Pastel blues, pinks and peach (especially for summer)	White, silver grey, lilac, slightly deeper shades of blue pink and peach, very light caramel or toffee brown

worn with lighter shoes. Black tights and red shoes are a striking combination, provided that they team with the rest of your outfit.

Bags. Handbags seem to come in all shapes and sizes. For everyday use, a larger, practical, satchel-style of bag, preferably in leather, is best. When you are dressing up, a smaller shoulder bag or clutch bag, is more suitable. Don't always think that your handbag has to match your shoes.

Gloves. Most women only wear gloves to keep their hands warm, and this is good enough reason to have a couple of pairs of woolly gloves – perhaps one patterned and one plain or one dark and one bright. But, as an investment buy, a pair of leather gloves does improve a smart outfit, so look out for reductions at sale time.

If you sensibly work through this list of items, you will end up with a very sound and flexible basic wardrobe. As the illustrations on these pages show, there, is a great deal you can do with it. However, one of the most important points about a carefully constructed basic wardrobe, is that you can build on it, economically and with confidence. Later chapters discuss in more detail the more specialised aspects, such as evening wear, smart clothes for special occasions, summer clothes, coats, and so on. But they all start from the same basic assumption. If the foundations are firm, the whole structure will work. Wise buying will save you a lot of money, time and disappointment; you will be able to say of your wardrobe that 'it all hangs together'.

Fabrics

Fabrics are all important. In fact, they are just as important as the style you choose to wear. And often, if you can afford to pay a little more for something, you will not only get a better cut, but a much higher quality of fabric will have been used.

Fabrics are particularly important when you are buying investment clothes, for example, the classic coat that will last you for several years or the favourite red sweater that will have a permanent place in your wardrobe. Natural fibres, like pure new wool—with its enormous range of weights and textures—and cashmere and silk, or fabrics with a high proportion of natural to man-made fibre, will not only last and wear well, but will look and feel good to wear. Obviously, man-made fabrics are cheaper, and some of them are excellent. But there is nothing to beat the touch of a pure silk shirt, or a cashmere sweater, even if it is a few years old.

Most of the clothes that the Princess of Wales took to Australia, Canada and New Zealand were made of silk, which, like cotton, is especially cool to wear in hot weather. Man-made fabrics don't seem to let the body breathe so easily and therefore tend to make you perspire more. It is well worth bearing this in mind, particularly for such occasions as summer weddings, or when on long 'plane journeys. This doesn't mean that you can only wear wool or silk, but try for instance to break down the layers of man-made fabrics you wear. Cotton underwear can help a good deal. Or choose a fabric with a high proportion of natural to man-made fibres, and get some of the best of both worlds.

The main drawback to these natural fibres is that they do tend to crease. Real linen for example seems to crease the minute you put it on. Sometimes the creases will fall out fairly quickly, but there is a better way of getting round the problem, which can be particularly useful on days when you have a great deal of travelling, sitting and standing to do: wear a patterned fabric. Somehow, creases do not show up as much on checks, floral patterns and stripes. This may be a complete optical illusion, but it is one that works. The very 'Highland' outfit designed by Caroline Charles which the Princess wore for the Braemar Games in September 1982 not only delighted everyone because of its strong Scottish influence but, being tartan, you could not see too many creases.

Fabric coordination

Mixing different fabrics together can produce a highly striking effect. One way of doing this is to match print and plain, but this need not be the only combination. However, if you are going to mix two patterned fabrics together, there are some simple guidelines to follow. Floral prints worn together can work in any of three ways. Firstly, if they are the same print, but in a different colourway. Secondly, where a matching print in a large and a small size is mixed together in the same colourway. Thirdly, where patterns recognisably belong to the same family; a large and small check can work together provided they are linked by, for example, colour. Marrying clothes of different textures together can also be very dynamic. Stylish dressers are quite likely to wear silk with heavy tweed, velvet with wool flannel, and leather with cashmere. Before you dismiss this as too extreme, take a look at your own wardrobe. If you have a tweed skirt or jacket, then why not wear it with a silk blouse or top instead of the usual heavy sweater or cotton shirt? Some good combinations are shown opposite.

Above; a tartan look for the Braemar Games in September 1982. An appropriate choice of fabric, not just for its 'Scottishness' but also for its ability to withstand creasing during long hours of sitting. It was designed by Caroline Charles. Facing page; rough fabrics with smoother, softer textures make an interesting combination. To make it work, you obviously have to make the heavier fabric your main one, coordinating it with the lighter fabric. Good and unusual combinations include leather with angora; wool suiting with satin; lace with wool crêpe; suede with brushed cotton; linen with silk chiffon; and cashmere with silk satin. Don't be afraid to experiment by buying or collecting some small swatches of fabric and seeing how they look together.

...printed satin with...

...leather with angora...

wool   suiting

...lace with denim...

...with heavy wool tweed...

...lace with cord...

...linen with silk chiffon...

crepe de chine

...with silk...

...suede

Health and beauty

There is little doubt that in order for anyone to emulate the kind of energy, glow and good looks that Princess Diana so consistently shows, they need a recipe of good health, enviable self-discipline and happiness.

Our looks betray the lives we lead. If we get insufficient sleep, smoke or drink to excess, over-indulge in the wrong foods or under-nourish our bodies—if we have no pride in our appearance—it shows in many ways. It might be in sallow, blotchy skin, dark or bloodshot eyes, or we may have an air of general sluggishness and lethargy, become obese or at the other extreme, anorexic.

Princess Diana's brand of beauty is a picture of health itself. She has that wide-awake, fresh and healthy appeal and a real zest for living. But despite her amazing metamorphosis from 'Shy Di' to dazzling Princess, her basic good looks were there from the start, though as a slightly overweight teenager with plain brown hair cut in rather a severe style, her potential wasn't always immediately obvious —except, perhaps, to her future husband.

Diana's much publicised weight loss has had a dramatic effect on her looks and has certainly revealed a beautiful bone structure. Marriage and childbirth have also brought a new dignity and composure to her face, whose beauty is now appreciated the world over.

While the Princess has clearly followed expert advice from top make-up artists such as Barbara Daly (whom you may recall created her lovely Wedding Day make-up, see page 115), she had a head start with many natural beauty assets. Let's first consider these:

1 Glossy, healthy hair, which London crimper Kevin Shanley has looked after and groomed for several years. Not a particularly remarkable style (although it has been copied the world over), but one which suits her, and that is Kevin Shanley's basic philosophy.

Most of us are born with healthy hair. But as we learn to 'abuse' it more and more with heated appliances, sun exposure, the wrong hair products, its condition begins to deteriorate.

By keeping hair close to natural, as Diana has largely done for most of her 22 years (though now she is much fairer), we stand a better chance of maintaining the bounce, elasticity and high-gloss of youth. (See the Hair section on page 28).

2 Peachy-clear complexion. Good skin is usually inherited, so you're jolly lucky if your ancestors had smooth complexions. But if the future of your skin concerns you, then look at your mother's and her mother's complexions—if they resemble a map of Great Britain, it's likely yours will take that route, too.

Every woman has some minor skin

problem that bothers her, and whilst Diana's complexion appears flawless, her high colouring must have bothered her on more than one occasion. (For more about skin, see page 34).

3 Good bone structure. This is something you either have or have not got. Diana's didn't really come to light until she lost weight and then learned how to make the most of her features with cosmetics. Many slimmers are amazed that weight goes so quickly from the face, and that when it does it often reveals a very good bone structure. We can't alter Nature, of course, but we can all improve on it with clever cosmetics. (See section on Make-up on pages 30–33).

4 A pair of sparkling blue eyes. Diana's genuinely twinkle when she smiles. The eyes really are the mirror of the soul. And you can smile and pose all you like for photographs, flashing your teeth and pulling your mouth back to your ears— but if the smile isn't genuine it will show in your eyes.

For eyes to look their best, the whites need to look almost blue-white. Smoking, pollution, alcohol and bright

sunlight are the eyes' worst enemies. Notice how smokers always frown as they draw on a cigarette and then squint as they blow smoke up in their own faces.

The dust and grit of a city makes our eyes sore, too. To soothe, give them a clear-water eye bath, an ice cold eye mask or add a few drops of soothing eye lotion.

In strong sunlight, it is very important to wear sunglasses as the Princess has done on many occasions. They not only shade the eyes and help prevent squinting, but they deflect the ultra violet rays that can actually do lasting damage to the eyes.

Excessive alcohol is harmful to the health and to the eyes because it dilates the blood vessels of the eyes, causing

them to look bloodshot. It also, in common with smoking, dehydrates the skin. Diana is not a 'big drinker' but she is reported to enjoy a glass of champagne (which puts a 'sparkle' in the eyes) and takes mineral water with her wine.

5 Good teeth that give a dazzling smile every time. Diana is clearly not afraid to show her perfect, gleaming teeth, otherwise, like so many people who are not proud of their teeth, she would smile with her mouth firmly shut.

Healthy teeth are basically a genetic gift and if your parents have their own, there's every chance yours will survive to a ripe old age.

Despite the genetics, it is important to encourage good dental care. Regular six-monthly visits to the dentist are essential. Teeth can be protected with a fluoride

toothpaste and by regular brushing with a firm brush that is renewed every two to three months.

Dental floss and antiseptic mouth washes also help keep the mouth clean and sweet.

6 Being tall has its advantages, although the way Diana stooped shyly in the early days suggested that she didn't find her 5 feet 8 inches an asset in the very least. She seems now to appreciate her graceful height, which allows her to wear stunning gowns which simply wouldn't work on short people. And she looks as though she enjoys being tall as she draws herself up to her full height with confidence. Of course, being tall and rather curvy as a teenager is completely different from being tall and very slender, which she now is.

Hair

We all aspire to a head of glossy, healthy hair with natural movement and plenty of body. Hair that's versatile, manageable and never lets us down. Sadly, most of us complain bitterly about our hair, it's generally too straight, too curly, won't behave, lacks volume and so on.

Princess Diana's hair is surely not trouble-free (she must have had 'those moments', too) but it never lets her down in public. Her hairdresser of several years, Kevin Shanley, has proved that one simple, basic cut is the most versatile cut of all. It's the cut which suits her, yet it has been flexible in the past couple of years and very accommodating.

As a teenager she wore it much shorter and rather flatter, framing her face. She hadn't ventured into the realms of multi-lighting at that time—but what a stunning impact her now much fairer hair has made. The basic, short cut she originally had, worn with a side parting, has been allowed to grow longer and become more voluminous. There's a softer, more feathered feel to the style, a direct result of layering and highlighting.

It is interesting that Diana has never been seen with her hair back off her forehead; she always keeps a full and heavy fringe, though it has more movement these days. It is possible that her face would take on a completely new look if she swept her hair back a little.

When Diana first appeared on the Royal scene, there was great consternation about her stylish hair cut. People were anxious that it wouldn't look 'Royal' enough and that she simply wouldn't be able to carry off the tiaras and crowns of a Princess and future Queen.

People needn't have worried. Our modern day Princess has proved that a tiara looks even more stunning on a beautiful head of healthy and stylish hair, than it sometimes does on more formally dressed hair.

Furthermore, not only does her lifestyle call for hats to complete her outfits, but Diana is a 'hat fiend' and must have worn just about every shape, colour and style imaginable—and all with great success.

There is one aspect of Diana's hair that is beautifully contrived, and that is the sweeping sideline which is clearly cut shorter to show off her splendid array of earrings. (See facing page.) Now a keen jewellery enthusiast, she has far surpassed her days of the golden 'Di' necklace and clearly adores every single piece she owns. Drop earrings are favourites with her and balance perfectly with her hairstyle. Other familiar choices are the diamond and sapphire drops she wore in her twenty-first portraits and her pear-shaped diamond drops with an interchangeable sapphire/ruby centre.

Being so closely and so consistently scrutinised makes it very difficult for her ever, quite literally, to have a 'hair out of place'. Whilst Diana's hair is probably quite fine and worn in a simple, uncontrived style, it never looks unruly, and even when windswept, it keeps its style and shape.

Quite what plans Mr Shanley has in mind for her hair, we cannot say. Perhaps he hasn't yet decided himself. But the way things are going, it's bound to grow longer and eventually one day, perhaps, we could see it elegantly styled in a modern-day twist. Husband Charles, of course, has always had a keen eye for feminine beauty, so it is unlikely that he will encourage Diana to grow her hair any shorter than it is now. A loose and flowing style—which would no doubt appeal more to him than chignons or tiaras—may yet be to come.

Hair care

Love and happiness have put the shine in Diana's eyes, but the shine on her hair comes from two things: healthy diet, and regular conditioning treatments.

The state of our hair reflects the state of our bodies. If we're ill, distressed or under-nourished, our hair will look lank, dull and lack bounce. When we're in top form, our hair usually shines, reflecting the light, and bounces.

Generally speaking a healthy diet that keeps the figure slim is also a good regime for the hair. But in particular the hair needs vitamins (especially B vitamins), minerals and protein. Avoid too much fat or carbohydrate.

Every day include lean meat or fish, fresh fruit, vegetables and/or green salad. Drink plenty of water and ensure supplies of vitamin B by eating liver, whole grain cereals, nuts and beans, or take Brewer's yeast tablets for extra vitamin B.

To maintain a good, healthy condition, hair should be washed with the right kind of shampoo for its type— dry, greasy or normal. And if it is shampooed very regularly, or even every day, then it must be done with a very mild, 'frequent use' shampoo which will not strip the natural oils from the hair and leave it dry.

After shampooing, hair should be blotted dry with a towel and then treated with a cream rinse or conditioner. This only needs about one minute to work on the hair as it simply coats the outer shaft to enable the cuticles to lie flat and reflect light. It is then rinsed off and the hair can be styled.

Every few weeks, the hair can be treated with a deep-action, more penetrating treatment, which actually gets inside the hair shaft and promotes longer lasting shine. Diana's favourite salon, for example, uses steam and massage treatment to maintain hair and scalp health.

Whenever a treatment is used on the hair, it's a good idea to wrap the hair with a polythene bag, then wrap again with a hot towel. The heat encourages the treatment to penetrate the hair and work more effectively.

There are many hair treatment packs from which to choose on the market, but warmed almond or olive oil works

wonders on dull hair, too. It needs to be thoroughly rinsed off after about one hour, though.

Conditioners also help to protect the hair from other influences, such as harsh weather and rough handling. Heated appliances such as hot brushes, tongs and blow dryers can be very bad for the hair as they tend to make it dry and brittle.

Diana's hair is probably styled with a blow dryer every day (certainly when she is appearing in public) but it won't harm the hair if the dryer is held about 12 inches away from the hair and if a protective blow-styling lotion is used.

It's a good habit to visit the hairdresser about every six weeks for a trim. This won't noticeably shorten the length of the hair, but cuts off all the dryish ends, eliminates any splits which can never be mended, but which do have a habit of running along the hair shaft to ruin the rest of the hair. Trimming brings new

life to a perm, and puts bounce into a flagging style. It also gives precision cuts, such as the bobs which are now so popular, a sharper, crisper outline.

Finally, how do you give your hair that touch of good grooming that is so characteristic of the Princess herself? Could it be that she has discovered the joys of the new setting gels and foam mousses? They work just like setting lotions to give a style staying power, yet they are non-sticky and much more versatile.

Hairspray, of course, will also hold a style in place—and today's sprays are firm enough to hold a style, yet soft enough to leave the hair looking like hair instead of concrete. The secret is to hold the can a good eight or ten inches away from the hair and just let a light spray fall gently over the hair. Brush it out at the end of the day and the hair bounces back perfectly.

Royal make-up

Diana's colouring is fairly typical of the English look. At times she can look delicately pale and needs the warmth of a blusher on her cheekbones. But when excited, emotional, under stress—or simply hot—her flushed complexion needs cooling down. In the early days Diana wore little or no make-up—quite normal for a girl with a fresh complexion and in her 'teens. She has learned to even out her skin tones more now by using a light textured, neutral toned foundation. (It should match closely with your facial skin tones, whether you're pale, rosy, olive, coffee toned or black—and you can mix shades to get the right tone. Never leave a distinction between face and throat.)

Face powder is now among her cosmetics, which as a kindergarten teacher she never used. A loose powder, applied lightly over foundation with cotton wool sets the base make-up, keeps shine at bay and gives a professional finish to her make-up. It also helps to camouflage a high cheek colouring.

Face shaping is a real art. If you get it right you can give your face an entirely new appeal. Get it wrong, however, and you can accentuate the features you are trying to minimise. In the early days Diana's face shape was undeniably round. Her short hair style seemed to emphasise the roundness and her country-fresh rosy complexion did little to minimise it, either. When she did use blusher, it wasn't always quite right. She often chose pink, which clashed badly as her cheek colouring rose. Today, as she's grown more poised and more confident, her colouring is less obvious. Possibly she does not colour up in the same way now, but equally, she has learned the art of make-up. Her face shape is now more oval/heart-shaped, her round cheeks have diminished and in their place are high cheekbones and more contoured cheeks. She opts for blushers in beautiful shades of peach and soft rust, the most complimentary for the skin. She also applies it high on her cheek bones to accentuate them, rather than towards the centre of her cheeks as she tended to when they least needed it.

With a few subtle changes, Diana's eye make-up has made a world of difference to her stunning blue eyes. In the past she had a penchant for blue eye shadow, attractive but perhaps a little obvious for her eye colour. And certainly 'safe' rather than adventurous. Since the Wedding, however, when top make-up artist Barbara Daly created a beautiful new look, the Princess has swopped her blues for browns, peaches and soft rust tones: still subtle and often understated, but very much more flattering and a perfect contrast for her blue eyes.

Apart from Gala occasions, which always call for slightly heavier make-up, Diana now applies her cosmetics with a lighter touch and has obviously learnt the art of blending over and over—a particular rule of Barbara Daly's, who owns hundreds of different cosmetic brushes to blend colour on every part of the face.

No make-up is complete without lip colour. It balances the total look and enhances the lip shape. Diana has quite full lips and wisely chooses soft, peachy or pale pink shades to colour them. Deep or very bright colours would exaggerate the fullness of her lips and could unbalance her make-up. She obviously prefers lip colour that is moist and has a sheen to it. She doesn't wear a high gloss, but a subtle one that gives the lips a lovely moist quality.

Diana's has been the most remarkable metamorphosis on Royal record. And the Princess has done it virtually by herself. The nice part is that, although she has changed so dramatically, she still remains natural, fresh, youthful and unspoilt. Long may she be so!

Facing page; an example of Royal make-up. Diana's foundation evens the skin tones yet is light enough to let the translucency of her skin show through. A light dusting of loose powder gives a matt finish and helps set the base. Cheekbones are enhanced with a peachy blusher blended well towards the outer edges of her face using a fat blusher brush. Her toning lip colour in a peachy shade has a hint of gloss to accompany the sparkle of her diamonds. Her long lashes are coloured with mascara and the lids are beautifully shaded with a perfect blend of gold to highlight brow-bones and lid curves, and brown in the socket area to add shape and depth to the lids.

Make-up

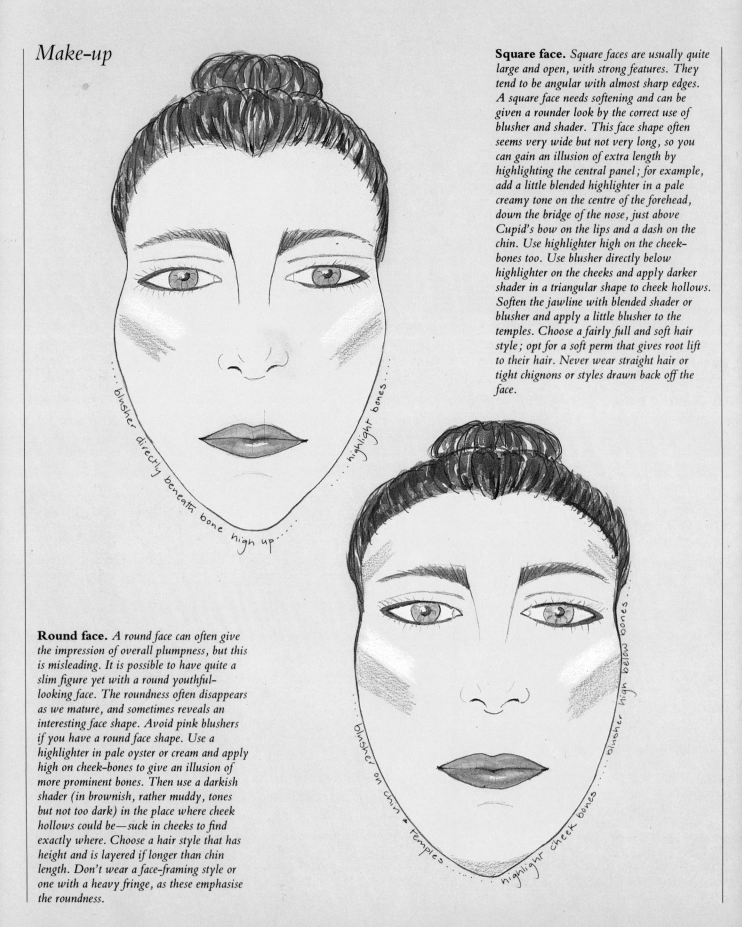

Square face. *Square faces are usually quite large and open, with strong features. They tend to be angular with almost sharp edges. A square face needs softening and can be given a rounder look by the correct use of blusher and shader. This face shape often seems very wide but not very long, so you can gain an illusion of extra length by highlighting the central panel; for example, add a little blended highlighter in a pale creamy tone on the centre of the forehead, down the bridge of the nose, just above Cupid's bow on the lips and a dash on the chin. Use highlighter high on the cheek-bones too. Use blusher directly below highlighter on the cheeks and apply darker shader in a triangular shape to cheek hollows. Soften the jawline with blended shader or blusher and apply a little blusher to the temples. Choose a fairly full and soft hair style; opt for a soft perm that gives root lift to their hair. Never wear straight hair or tight chignons or styles drawn back off the face.*

Round face. *A round face can often give the impression of overall plumpness, but this is misleading. It is possible to have quite a slim figure yet with a round youthful-looking face. The roundness often disappears as we mature, and sometimes reveals an interesting face shape. Avoid pink blushers if you have a round face shape. Use a highlighter in pale oyster or cream and apply high on cheek-bones to give an illusion of more prominent bones. Then use a darkish shader (in brownish, rather muddy, tones but not too dark) in the place where cheek hollows could be—suck in cheeks to find exactly where. Choose a hair style that has height and is layered if longer than chin length. Don't wear a face-framing style or one with a heavy fringe, as these emphasise the roundness.*

32

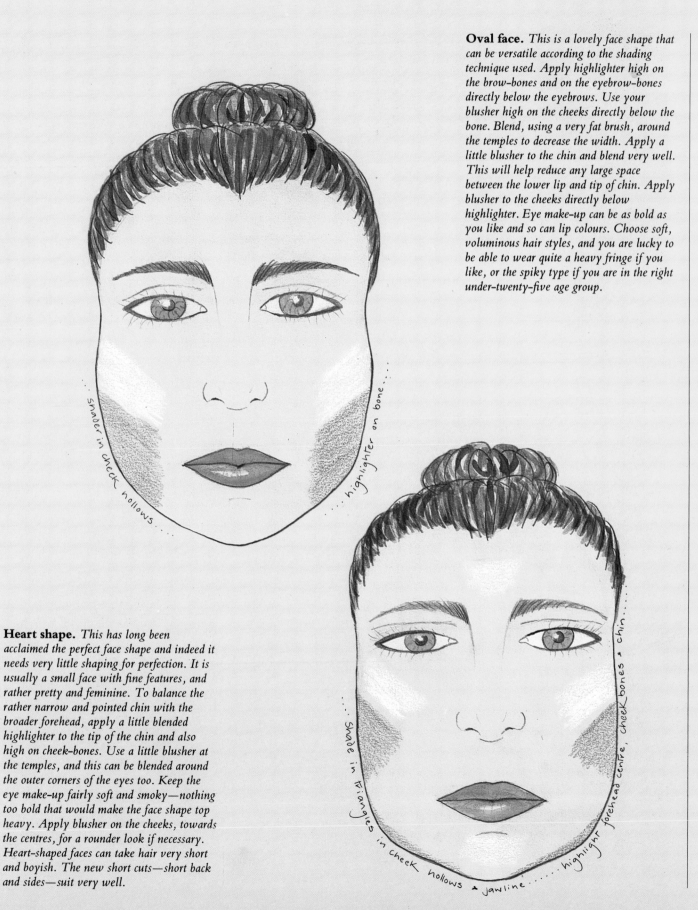

Shader in cheek hollows.....

.....highlighter on bone.....

Oval face. *This is a lovely face shape that can be versatile according to the shading technique used. Apply highlighter high on the brow-bones and on the eyebrow-bones directly below the eyebrows. Use your blusher high on the cheeks directly below the bone. Blend, using a very fat brush, around the temples to decrease the width. Apply a little blusher to the chin and blend very well. This will help reduce any large space between the lower lip and tip of chin. Apply blusher to the cheeks directly below highlighter. Eye make-up can be as bold as you like and so can lip colours. Choose soft, voluminous hair styles, and you are lucky to be able to wear quite a heavy fringe if you like, or the spiky type if you are in the right under-twenty-five age group.*

.....Shade in triangles in cheek hollows & jawline.....

.....highlight forehead centre, cheek bones & chin.....

Heart shape. *This has long been acclaimed the perfect face shape and indeed it needs very little shaping for perfection. It is usually a small face with fine features, and rather pretty and feminine. To balance the rather narrow and pointed chin with the broader forehead, apply a little blended highlighter to the tip of the chin and also high on cheek-bones. Use a little blusher at the temples, and this can be blended around the outer corners of the eyes too. Keep the eye make-up fairly soft and smoky—nothing too bold that would make the face shape top heavy. Apply blusher on the cheeks, towards the centres, for a rounder look if necessary. Heart-shaped faces can take hair very short and boyish. The new short cuts—short back and sides—suit very well.*

The complexion

Having a flawless complexion is something that Diana probably takes for granted. She has the country-fresh looks of a woman who needs to do little more than wash her face and add a touch of light moisturiser. Having a good skin really is one of the most wonderful beauty assets. Somehow it gives confidence to a woman and it is most definitely essential if make-up is to look its best.

Good skin is usually passed down the family, but once we have it, we must learn how to keep it. The wrong treatment can ruin it as the years go by. Although the Princess's skin looks as though it needs little pampering, it is highly likely that Diana is as keen as any of us to hang on to her fresh looks and to keep the elasticity of youth. She has therefore probably learned how to care for her skin in such a way that it not only looks good now, but will stay that way for long into the future. She may well be a 'soap and water' person, especially since her skin is prone to shine on occasions. Water helps to dry the skin slightly so is ideal for more oily complexions. Today's soaps are known as 'cleansing bars'. They look and work like soap, but are specially designed not to leave any deposits on the skin and most barely lather at all.

Not all of us are fortunate enough to have a complexion as fresh as Diana's. Some skins are delicate and sensitive, and prone to broken veins in the cheeks which will give an unwelcome high colour. Other skins are dry and likely to wrinkle far earlier than others. And still other skins, perhaps the most troublesome of all, are oily and suffer from blemishes and spots, particularly in adolescence. Whatever the condition of your skin, there are certain precautions you can take to minimise the damage. If you have a particularly sensitive skin, for example, you should avoid curries and other spicy foods, and alcohol. If you have to face harsh weather, make sure that you are protected by plenty of moisturiser and a good protective foundation. Dry skins will need plenty of lubrication—moisturiser during the day and special light-textured night creams at night. Oily skins will benefit from steam treatments, washing with special soaps, and facial masks every three to five days rather than once a week.

Skin care

A person with Diana's skin type could follow a regime that included a cleansing bar face wash in the morning, followed by a slightly astringent lotion and a very light moisturiser for normal/combination skin. This is the type which has an oily or shiny central panel down nose, forehead and chin, and is slightly drier on the cheeks. At night, she would need something richer to remove the day's make-up. There are many excellent cleansing creams formulated for combination and more oily skins. If water was still preferred to a tissue-off cream, then a cream and water product could be used. This is the type which is often rich and creamy when massaged over the face, but which is rinsed off with water rather than tissued.

This would be followed again by a skin tonic, which removes last traces of cleanser and helps tighten and firm the skin. After this a light night cream will moisturise the skin and over the years will help stave off the first signs of dehydration and the inevitable wrinkles.

No matter how thoroughly we cleanse our skin, it is always necessary to have a deep-cleanse on a weekly basis with one of the many face packs or the new facial scrubs. These usually contain crushed seeds or almond meal which are slightly abrasive to the skin and help slough off dead skin cells. They also help refine the pores and minimise spots and blemishes. And they leave the skin feeling silky soft and with that wonderful translucent, reflective quality that Diana's skin has.

The value of a good complexion is enormous. It is interesting to compare this picture with the one on the previous page; we can see the transformation of the pretty rather round-faced girl into the elegant, mature and beautiful woman of today.

Diet and exercise

Every woman who has ever been overweight and conscious of it knows how it feels to be criticised by others. But most of us only have to contend with husbands, lovers, relations and friends. Imagine how it must feel to have the eyes of the world focused on you, describing you in 'homely' terms and commenting on your round face and sweet tooth. It was hardly surprising that Diana got the message and very quickly did something about it.

There are those who have said that she went too far, but a lot of us believe that she has never looked better. Now, she can afford to gain a little weight, as most dieters can when they level-off. Nobody knows the details of Diana's diet story, but she enjoys healthy eating with crisp salads, vegetables and fresh fruit. She does have a sweet tooth (as her own favourite recipe for fudge bears witness!) but she has obviously learned to curb and control it, proving that sweet-toothed people can still lose weight. One helpful method is to reward oneself at the end of each diet day with a little sweetness, such as a small plain biscuit, one cube of chocolate or one sweet. There are also special dieting aids based on sweetness so that a slimmer can satisfy her 'weakness' and still lose weight. The one thing a sweet-toothed person should never do is deprive herself of sugar. This only brings about a craving for it and that does not make sound dieting philosophy.

The key to sensible eating and long-term weight maintenance is on the lines of Her Majesty the Queen's own philosophy to 'eat a *little* of everything'. To reject everything would be insensitive and unsociable, whereas to eat absolutely everything would surely lead to obesity. If the Royal Family can manage to stay slim with all the exotic culinary delights set before them, then surely it's possible for the rest of us to eat just a small portion of everyday foods?

Dieting has become such a desperate business today that we have almost lost track of the essence of healthy eating. Deprivation does make us slim. But if we can't live normal, sociable lives eating a balanced mixture of food, then we have won a very hollow victory.

Dieting makes us slim, but only exercise can tone and firm those lazy muscles to make us supple and shapely. Diana's enthusiasm for swimming, the best all-round form of exercise, dancing (she was an avid tap dancer in pre-William days) and exercise to music has stood her in good stead for her demanding roles as Princess of Wales, wife and mother. She positively snapped back into shape after the birth of Prince William and no doubt followed her post-natal exercises determinedly. The women who don't do this are those who suffer most later with flabbiness, floppiness and such unmentionables as 'dropped pelvic floors'.

Aerobics have brought new meaning to the word 'exercise' and Diana is apparently an enthusiast of the Californian style work-outs which Jane Fonda initiated. Aerobics certainly get every part of the body tingling and the blood circulating, and there's plenty of puffing and panting to the throb of the pop beat. This is the type of workout that's done in classes and centres countrywide, but there are also books, records and videos available for those who wish to leap about in the privacy of their own home.

The term 'aerobic' has come to mean 'dynamic exercise to pop music' loosely speaking, but in fact it refers to any form of oxygenating exercise such as jogging, dancing and swimming. Aerobics are strictly for the healthy and fairly fit, definitely not advisable for the very creaky, mature, rank beginners who have never exercised, nor, obviously, for those under medical supervision. To experience a taste of what it could be like, put on a fast-beat pop record then leap up and down, from side to side and kick your legs high in the air about ten times for the full three minutes. Exhilarating isn't it!

Alternatively, for those wishing to whittle away an inch or so whilst toning their tummies and firming the flab, there are more gentle exercises that can be done morning, noon or night, whenever there's a spare five minutes—dumb-bell exercises, for example, or sit-ups to firm up the tummy muscles.

Whether you choose to run, dance, swim, weight-lift or whatever, the main thing about exercise is to do it regularly (at least twice a week), choose the type of exercise that you'll enjoy and not one you feel obliged to do, to start gently and increase pace gradually—and to keep at it.

CHAPTER TWO

Everyday Wear

The Princess off duty. Diana gets few opportunities to dress informally, but these cropped trousers and shirt, with a sweater draped over the shoulders, are very casual and relaxed.

A pair of cropped trousers, a plain shirt and a sweater tied casually round the neck: these are not the clothes that we would normally associate with the Princess of Wales. And indeed the Princess has few chances, at least in public, to wear the sort of casual everyday clothes that most young women of her age would be seen in much of the time. There are occasional polo matches, infrequent holidays and a few more relaxed public engagements which allow her to break away from the rather formal style that is usually demanded of her, but it is not often that she can forget the demands of her Royal image and wear an outfit for the simple reason that she enjoys wearing it. This is, perhaps, one of the few areas in which other women have a distinct advantage over the Princess. This is even more true now than it was before. There is a new approach to casual clothes. Newer because it is more coordinated but at the same time less restricting in style, making the clothes easy and comfortable to wear. The new casuals are not only for wearing at home, or for a stroll in the country, but for work as well.

It is fascinating to speculate about the clothes that the Princess wears during her rare moments of privacy. But if the examples of her more casual style that we have had a chance to see are anything to go by, her sense of style and of fashion is as strong in this area as in any other. An interesting example is the tweedy check jacket with matching skirt designed by Bill Pashley, which Diana wore at Balmoral not long after the wedding. Jackets and skirts that match, or coordinate, are more casual than a smart tailored suit and make ideal outfits for everyday wear. The Princess's outfit has rather a 'country' feel to it because of the fabric and the casual styling of the blouson style jacket and the front pleated skirt. This, in fact, is a very versatile outfit. The jacket would look good with a plain gathered skirt or culottes, or even jeans. The skirt would look good with a blouse, sweater, or a more tailored, plain coloured, blazer.

One of the biggest influences on the casual clothes scene has been sportswear. Sporty-styled clothes might be better called 'spectator' clothes these days, since they have spread far beyond the bounds of the sports field. Tracksuits, baseball t-shirts and running shorts are just a few of the styles that have been incorporated into fashionable dress. Trackwear, or rather 'sweatwear', is readily available in a variety of styles and colours, from the basic top and pants to gilets (large waist-coats), skirts and dresses. There are also the 'keep fit' influenced looks. Clothes like leotards, footless tights and leg warmers, which used to belong in the gym or the dance studio, have become part of our everyday wardrobe. Because of the new interest in healthy living and keeping fit, clothes have been adapted to move with the body rather than restricting it. Princess Diana is reputed to swim and dance regularly, so the Royal wardrobe no doubt contains clothes of this style too.

Another new development has been the introduction of a more layered style of dressing, giving what might be called an 'ethnic' look. Nowadays, many casual clothes are more unstructured—or less tailored and shaped—than they used to be. Again, the look is coordinated as well as comfortable—gone are the rather scruffy and haphazard looks of the '70s—and also very practical. You can

Facing page; Prince Charles and the Princess of Wales meet the world's press just after their marriage. Prince Charles wears a Balmoral tartan and Diana a hound's-tooth check suit designed by Bill Pashley.

38

remove a layer or two when coming indoors from outside, and add them back on if the weather takes a turn for the worse. The parts look as good as the whole. Such fashion rules as exist are often successfully ignored in this style of dressing. Wear your skirt over leggings, and a sleeveless sweater with a shirt or t-shirt underneath and a jacket and gilet over the top. Then throw a shawl or scarf over the lot. By coordinating colours and textures, this casual approach can look very fashionable and stylish.

Winter clothes

Casual clothes for winter, such as skirts, tops, sweaters, pants and jackets, are in many ways year-round clothes, at least in a climate like Britain's. This is particularly true of separates, and separates that coordinate not only in colour but in fabric and style are the best clothes to use as the basis for an everyday wardrobe. Winter clothes will, of course, tend to be in warmer fabrics—woollen fabrics and brushed cotton rather than silk or plain cotton—and warmer, darker colours seem more appropriate. A good winter outfit would be a soft wool skirt with a brushed cotton patterned blouse, teamed with a sleeveless slipover or waistcoat in a colour that coordinates with the blouse and skirt. The colours don't have to match exactly; a rust coloured slipover would go well with a brown skirt and a rust, cream and brown patterned blouse. Choose your colours and textures carefully so that they work together, and try unusual combinations from time to time, not always the obvious ones. (See page 24 for Fabric coordination).

Coats

A major item in a winter wardrobe, and very likely the most expensive one, is a coat. Cheap coats can, of course, be bought, but they tend to look shabby after a single season's wear. A good coat is worth saving for. This does mean, however, that you need to give quite a lot of thought to the sort of coat you want before you go out and buy it. Dark or bright in colour, fitted or loose in cut, classic in style or a little more modern, the choice is up to you; but do be practical about it because you will be wearing it quite a lot.

The most classic of all is the double-breasted coat, very similar in style to a man's overcoat. It looks good in basic, neutral colours like navy and black, or in brighter colours with a dark trim. Heavy tweeds or herringbones will give it a more countrified look. If you are buying this coat in a plain colour, then it is more important than ever to invest in a good fabric. Somehow, in a cheaper cloth, these plain colours, particularly navy, black, grey or camel, tend to wear badly and very quickly look shabby.

The Princess of Wales wore a coat in this style, designed by the Chelsea Design Company, when she visited a children's playground in Kennington in December 1982. There is a lot of fashion detail in this particular example. The bright red coat has large buttons, velvet revers and turn-up cuffs in contrasting black (see also page 44). The Princess wore a similar coat, but with a more military styling, during her Canadian tour. In the style of the Chelsea Design Company, in bright blue and black, it was elegant and particularly eye-catching for a dull winter's day. This is a style that works well in longer rather than shorter lengths.

Diana shows her taste for bright colours, even for heavy winter coats. This electric blue coat, with black velvet stand-up collar and matching trim on pockets and cuffs, proves the point. It was worn to visit Carbonear in Newfoundland, Canada, in June 1983.

Above; the Snow Princess, in Cossack-style coat with matching hat and muff, designed by Belville Sassoon. This visit to Gloucester Cathedral in December 1981 took place on the coldest day of the year. Above right; this cashmere coat by Caroline Charles was first worn in Carmarthen in 1981, and again during the Royal tour of New Zealand in 1983—a good coat for spring and autumn wear.

These slim-fitting coats always look smart, and they go well with trousers as well as with skirts and dresses. Accessories should follow through the same colour scheme. A casual hat, like a beret or a pull-on beanie style, would be more stylish than an ordinary scarf.

For more complicated styles, plain rather neutral colours often work well. For example, the cossack-style coat that the Princess wore to Gloucester Cathedral in December 1981 was in grey throughout—including the accessories. Warm but very stylish, this coat was designed by Bellville Sassoon in flannel trimmed with astrakhan, and with a frog-fastening front. The outfit was completed by a hat and muff. It is an indication of the Princess's influence that, a few days after she wore this coat, Harrods was inundated with requests for muffs. For everyday wear, the hat and muff could be exchanged, with almost as much effect, for a close-fitting knitted woollen pull-on hat and matching woolly gloves, either in grey or in a stronger, brighter colour. The Princess's burgundy leather boots are not only practical but the right choice for this outfit.

If you want a coat that is more appropriate for spring and autumn than for deep mid-winter, you will need something that is not too heavy or overstyled. Here again, the Princess provides us with a good model. She has worn, on several occasions, a lightweight camel wrapover coat, designed by Caroline Charles. Made in cashmere, a first class coat fabric, it has a shawl collar, slightly puff sleeves with a turn-back cuff, and a tie-belt fastening. This is a coat that would look good with soft frills or, less formally, with cord and tweed separates.

Even the Royal couple could not make the sun shine on their visit to a boating centre near Auckland in 1983. The rain was not allowed to dampen their spirits as the Princess covered-up with a classic style raincoat, similar in styling to a Burberry.

Raincoats are an obvious, and usually cheaper, alternative to a winter coat. They have the advantage that they can be used throughout the year, and they may fit better with your existing wardrobe. Ideally you should have both.

The choice of styles is enormous. At one end of the scale is the classic trench-coat in a neutral colour. This always looks good and is never likely to go out of fashion. It is one of the best of the investment buys. At the other end of the scale is the 'fun' mac in a shiny fabric and bright colours, featuring the latest fashion detail. And there is almost every variation in between. Even raincoats have taken on a more glamorous feel recently with the new fur-lined or fleecy-lined macs, which can look extremely elegant.

Princess Diana's choice of a raincoat is, of course, restricted by the need to wear something suitable for the occasion. So, for example, for a wet walkabout in Auckland, we see her wearing a rather classic style, fairly loose fitting mac with a checked lining and hood. This is a raincoat that could be thrown over any style of dress, and would suit more or less any everyday casuals.

Arabella Pollen is one of the youngest designers to have worked with the Princess. She, too, goes for simple styles in good fabrics. This elegant coat dress, together with another of similar style (see page 16), were part of her winter collection a few seasons ago and were picked out by the Princess. Ideal for an autumn walkabout, Diana wore this camel-check coat dress with a double-breasted fitted bodice and soft gathered skirt in Wales in November 1982. The soft leather trim around the neck, cuffs and for the buttons is followed through into the choice of accessories – low-heeled brown leather boots with heavy gauntlet style gloves, and a very soft suede beret. Note how the longer hemline suits this particular style of dress. A little warmer than an ordinary dress and a good alternative to a suit, the coat dress can be either casual or smart. It is ideal for cooler weather when the temperature doesn't demand a coat or jacket. And it can be worn indoors or out, depending on the fabric. Because of its style, a wool flannel or a suiting fabric like Prince of Wales check, or even corduroy, can all make an elegant coat dress.

Adapting the style

One of the most important items in your winter wardrobe is a coat. The chances are that you will get a lot of wear out of it, and it will need to serve the highly practical purpose of keeping you warm. It is worth spending money on a coat. Good fabrics and classic styles will see you through a good many winters, and you will have something you actually want to wear. One of the best choices, particularly if you can only afford one, is a classic double-breasted coat, like the one the Princess wore to visit the Charlie Chaplin adventure playground in Kennington, London, in December 1982. Designed by the Chelsea Design Company, the coat is made in a bright red wool with velvet trim. Adapting this basic shape can make it flattering for any figure.

Hourglass. Your shape gives you a choice of style. Either keep the look clean-cut with sharp contrasting detail, or go for a more belted design providing it isn't too tight or figure-hugging. Because of the bulky fabrics used for coats, a wrapover or any figure-skimming shape can make you look fatter. A collar or revers is fine as long as you don't go for anything too big. The simpler the style of coat you choose, the more you can afford to go for detail on the pockets, the collar or cuffs. Keep away from hairy or furry fabrics.

plain revers

plain cuff and pocket trim

plain collar

half belt

Pear shaped. Your best bet is a simply-cut coat – almost an overcoat style – or its opposite, a circular shape. Wrapovers with tie-belts only tend to emphasise your hips. Keep the front of the coat very simple with a clean-cut collar or revers. The top of your coat can be in a stronger or contrasting style to balance your bigger hips. You can, of course, afford to wear a high neckline, but be careful not to have the buttons too low down onto the hips. A clever adaptation is to go for a pleat back that will make the coat easier over the hipline without emphasising it. A simple half-belt would be a good additional detail. Never have too much pocket detail or large, shaped, pockets. The choice of colour and fabric is entirely a matter of individual taste.

Short-waisted. Coats are no different from dresses—at least as far as this shape is concerned. Any style that is tied or belted at the waist will unbalance your shape and emphasise your short waist. Either a simple double-breasted coat or a full circular shape would suit you. Sometimes the more simple and plain the style the more attractive it looks. A coat that has very large cuff trims which tend to fall in line with the 'normal' waist height can be a clever detail.

Top heavy. A coat that buttons right up to the neck or has any high collar detail such as a frill, or one that has over large buttons, will tend to emphasise the bustline. So too will a coat that is on a yoke. For collar detail go for revers or a shawl collar, preferably not in a contrasting colour or fabric. Either single or double-breasted styles will do, providing that the buttoning starts below the bustline. Steer clear of belted or tied waistlines – in fact, wrapover coats aren't very flattering at all. This simple double-breasted style would suit you either three-quarter length, or longer, depending on your height. Colours and fabrics are up to you but it is wise to keep away from strong contrast, especially on revers or collars.

Knitwear

Knitwear has come a long way since the twinset and pearl days of the 1930s and the figure hugging look of the 1950s when the sweater girl was born. Today, knitted looks in everything, from basic tops to skirts, dresses and coats, have become part of our everyday wardrobe. Knitwear has become much more design conscious and fashion orientated, and spans a very wide spectrum of styles.

The great number of styles available can sometimes make it difficult to choose, but you still need to make a choice before you buy, just as you would with any other garment. Sweaters, for example, seem to come in endless variety. In fine knits, they can be plain, lacy, fluffy, ribbed and even trimmed with leather or suede. They can be short, square-shaped and wider-cut, or they can be long and slim. They can be sleeveless or with batwing sleeves; round, roll or v-necked. And this is only a few of the variations available. Knitted clothes, particularly sweaters, also come in a great range of moods, from the rather classic styles to the chunky tweed knits. Old favourites include the roll-neck fisherman's style sweater that goes so well with tweedy skirts, and the more classic guernsey for wearing with jeans or cords. Both of these have a place in any wardrobe.

Diana's 'Black Sheep' sweater is convincing proof of her taste for beautiful, bold figurative knitwear. Made by a company called 'Warm and Wonderful', this simple round-neck drop-shoulder jumper is knitted in red, black and white three-ply pure wool. The young owners, Jo Osborne and Sally Muir, are delighted with the success this jumper has achieved. As Sally Muir tells us, 'it is hand-framed and hand-finished—including the dots for the sheep's eyes.'

Diana at Balmoral before the wedding, in the colourful sweater that she bought from Inca, a shop in Pimlico, London. An old favourite of Diana's, she used to wear it with a pair of jeans at the Kensington kindergarten where she worked.

Hand-knits or 'hand-made' sweaters, especially the intriguingly patterned ones and the 'fun' picture sweaters, have become more and more popular. Nowadays, you don't have to knit one yourself. This type of sweater can be bought in specialist knitwear shops as well as many high street chain stores. The prices range from the expensive designer knits to the much cheaper fashion ranges.

This surge of interest in knitwear has not escaped Diana's alert fashion eye. She, too, has been seen wearing distinctive and colourful patterned sweaters, even when she was pregnant, as well as her classic cashmeres. One was the charming 'weather' sweater showing clouds, lightning and rain which she wore with a pair of jeans to a polo match at Windsor. Another, worn on a similar occasion, again with a pair of jeans, was the intriguing 'black sheep' sweater designed by Warm and Wonderful. These must have made a pleasant distraction for any spectators bored by the polo. A further example was the bright 'Peruvian' sweater that she wore for a weekend walk with the Prince of Wales at Balmoral before their marriage. Here, in cords and 'wellies' she looks entirely relaxed.

Knitwear is not confined to chilly, wintry days. Super cotton knits in soft subtle colours and patterns look marvellous with lightweight printed or plain skirts, as well as with shorts and pants. Sleeveless vest tops with low backs, and easy wrapover sweaters are all styles that are now available in knitwear. They make excellent and stylish alternatives to t-shirts.

Winter casuals

Three important ways of wearing your winter clothes were mentioned at the beginning of the chapter: coordinates; sporting casuals; and the layered or 'ethnic' look. Here are some suggestions as to how you should wear each of these looks, and how you should incorporate them into your basic wardrobe.

Sporting casuals are some of the most comfortable clothes to wear. A simple track-suit looks very stylish with a quilted gilet, a scarf worn around the neck as a muffler, calf-warmers (half the length of leg-warmers) and matching knitted gloves and pull-on hat. Keep your jewellery to a minimum—a watch and plain stud earrings.

Coordinates will allow you a great deal of versatility since it is easy to up-grade them to a smarter look if necessary. Try a narrow collar shirt with a matching soft dirndl skirt, and a plain slipover (sleeveless jumper) in a co-ordinating colour. Choose opaque, slightly thicker tights that again co-ordinate with your sweater and your shoes. Add a narrow belt around the waist, and take a looser-shaped three-quarter length jacket to wear on top. A brooch or pin at the neck and matching earrings are the right accessory touch.

The 'ethnic' layers are often a little more complicated to put together. Start with a full circular skirt, with 'thermal' or thicker tights, or even 'combinations' for a warm underlayer. Wear this with a warmer fabric shirt (in brushed cotton for example), an Aran knit style of waistcoat or wider-shaped sweater, and round the whole outfit off with a large shawl scarf, almost a cape, on top. A wide leather belt, worn low on the hips, keeps this look rather unstructured and not too restricting. Low mid-calf boots would look good, and antique jewellery —slightly heavy earrings and a bangle— would have the right feel to them.

Winter accessories

Most women choose their everyday accessories for practical rather than fashion reasons. Of course, you don't want to be bothered with loads of beads around your neck while you are out shopping, or jangling beads when you are busy typing. But accessories can add a touch of style to even the most casual outfits provided that you don't overdo it and mix too many styles together.

Jewellery. For every day, you can get away with cheaper, more fun, jewellery, such as coloured wooden beads, bangles, earrings and pins. Rather bolder jewellery often works quite well. Good costume jewellery is a reliable stand-by; silver, gold, pearls and other semi-precious stones, real or fake, are a safe choice. A good watch, with a clear face, is practical and stylish.

Belts. Casual clothes will take such fashion styles as studded, jewelled and 'cowboy' belts. Cheaper materials, for example canvas, plastic and even rubber, can be used, so that you can afford to buy a selection of different colours.

Hats. A beret, a knitted pull-on and even a trilby, are useful styles to own. They will do for most occasions unless you need to look very smart.

Scarves. Long, short, square and shawl-sized scarves are all ideal to coordinate with any clothes, including casual ones. They don't just keep you warm. They can be tied, twisted or draped in any number of different ways. Try twisting a long scarf not too tightly around the neck to wear with a round-neck sweater or sweatshirt.

Tights. Make sure you have some slightly heavier knitted tights, and ones in opaque colours. It is well worth adding socks, leg-warmers and calf-warmers, especially in soft pastels or bright vivid colours.

Bags. For most of us, a small clutch bag isn't big enough for everyday clutter. A satchel type of shoulder bag is best.

Shoes. You will probably need a simple pump with either a flat or a medium heel. A trainer or plimsoll is good with sporty track-wear. For boots, the selection is vast but, in general, lower-cut 'baggy' boots look better with longer casual skirts and trousers, whereas the high straight-cut boots look better with the shorter lengths.

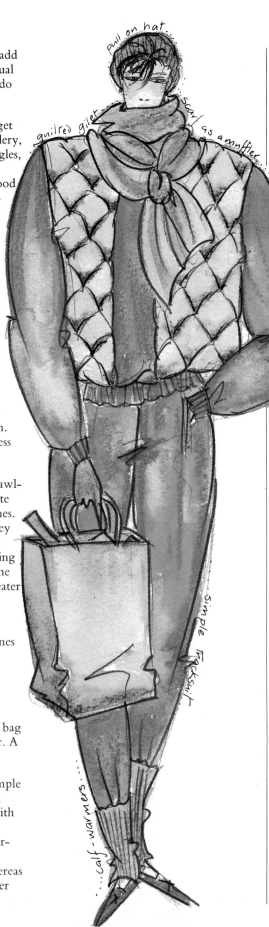

pull on hat

scarf as a muffler

quilted gilet

simple tracksuit

...calf-warmers...

full circular skirt

plain pullover

loose ¾ length jacket

dirndl skirt

thick opaque tights

Summer clothes

Summer fashion is as fickle as the weather itself. In retrospect, every summer seems perfect. Arms and legs, backs and shoulders, tanned to a golden brown by the summer sun, are set off by cool and pretty summer frocks. Memory turns the summer into a succession of long hot afternoons, lazy days by the sea and picnics in flower-filled fields. The reality is likely to be rather different. Nothing dates as fast as summer fashion and nothing is more elusive than the summer sun. For all its appeal, therefore, summer is the time when you need to be most practical about your clothes. Rushing out on the first warm sunny day to buy strapless tops, cotton skirts and open sandals is a mistake. Your first consideration should be your everyday clothes; high summer styles come second.

The Royal tour of Australia and New Zealand gave us plenty of opportunities to see the Princess's style of summer dressing. As always, she is practical, sensible and stylish. At no stage did we see a perspiring Princess. Her outfits followed all the major rules of dressing for warmer weather; they were cool, comfortable and not too tight. Wearing clothes that are too tight can be a serious mistake. They will make you hotter and you will look and feel uncomfortable. This applies to sleeves, armholes, bust and hips as much as to the waist. Cool, lightweight fabrics are obviously a help too. Cottons (in various weights from lawn to drill), silk and some mixes like cotton jersey, are all fabrics that breathe with the body and help cut down on perspiration. There is, of course, no point in choosing cool fabrics for your clothes, and then wearing nylon underwear. Cotton underwear and petticoats are much more comfortable to wear in hot weather. And not wearing a bra is not the right answer either. A drooping bust under a t-shirt is more unattractive than alluring. These days, with soft shaped bras that can be worn with strapless tops and low backed sweaters, there is no need for such discomfort.

The different styles of dressing for summer are very similar to those for winter. Coordinates, sportswear and layered looks are all as appropriate to warm weather as to cold. Coordinates for summer are ideal, and considerably more versatile than a summer dress. A good choice is a printed top or blouse with a skirt that matches or links in colour. One of the Princess's most stylish recent looks was Jan Vanvelden's blouse with pencil skirt and black leather cummerbund, worn at a Polo match in the summer of 1983. The simple addition of a white jacket would turn this into a very smart summer outfit. Or choose a blouse that can be worn open and give it an informal jacket look by wearing a t-shirt or camisole underneath. The soft white blouse and toning skirt designed by Benny Ong, which the Princess wore at Tennant Creek in Australia, is very much this sort of outfit. The jacket could very easily be worn open, with a vest or camisole underneath to give an entirely different look. Another example from the Royal wardrobe is the floral three-piece designed by Donald Campbell, which the Princess wore on her honeymoon. (See page 54 for further details.)

More conventional summer suits can also be effective. The navy blue sailor-style suit that Diana wore for a polo match at Windsor could be worn as either a smart or a casual outfit. The mood of a simple two-piece can easily be altered by wearing it with different blouses or tops. This particular style, designed by Belville Sassoon, is in the rather classic colour combination of navy, white and red, and would be suitable for a wide variety of occasions.

Sportswear and sports influenced clothes can be just as comfortable in summer as in winter. Obviously, you will need fewer layers, and shorts or skirts rather than

The Princess looked cool and casual in this soft white blouse and toning skirt, designed by Benny Ong, on a visit to the Karguru School in Australia in March 1983.

Above; the nautical-style outfit designed for Diana by Belville Sassoon. It was this outfit that she chose to wear for the official photograph with Prince Charles and the Queen, when the Privy Council approved the forthcoming marriage. Right; more than two years later, a rather different-looking Princess wears the latest high street fashion with very striking effect — a black and white blouse designed by Jan Vanvelden, a straight skirt and a leather cummerbund.

pants. Never wear tights under a tracksuit. They will make your legs feel as if they were bursting.

Softer, more feminine, layering of clothes has again become a fashionable way of wearing summer separates. Fashion trends come and go; sometimes a petticoat shows below the hem of the skirt and sometimes it doesn't; lacy trimmed blouses give way to grandad vest tops; skirts are frilled or not frilled, in fabrics that are either patterned or plain. But whatever the changing winds of fashion may bring, the basic style remains the same. Cheap imports of foreign fabrics, particularly from India, have added a touch of the exotic to this style of dressing.

Finally, a dress (whether for winter or summer) can make a refreshing change from separates and more casual clothes. Summer fashions change, but simple-cut,

Two summer holiday looks worn by a carefree Princess. Above; watching polo in a pair of yellow cotton dungarees with a large quilted bag. Above right; Bermuda shorts and white blouse, topped with a simple straw hat that perfectly reflects the holiday and honeymoon mood.

non-fuss styles never date so quickly. The white button-through dress designed by Benny Ong that the Princess wore for a visit to Ayers Rock in Australia, is just the sort of style to keep its appeal for several summers. In fact, white is the one summer colour that never goes out of fashion—probably because most women like to get a suntan, and nothing sets off a tanned skin so effectively as white. The Princess demonstrated the value of white on white on another occasion, wearing bermuda shorts and a cotton blouse as a pretty alternative to a t-shirt. The simple straw hat she wore perfectly suits the holiday mood.

These glimpses of the Princess in her 'off duty' cloths are refreshing, and always fun. It is nice to know that the future Queen of England likes, occasionally, to wear zany cotton dungarees and carry around a large floral quilted bag. The choice is still a practical and sensible one—cotton dungarees make a more colourful and cooler alternative to denims and a t-shirt, and busy mothers, among many others, would do well to copy it—but most important of all, it reminds us that the Princess is human. She is not just a public symbol of the monarchy; she is a cheerful, warm and pretty young woman.

It is hard to imagine anyone looking cooler or more elegant amidst the heat of Australia's Ayers rock than the Princess of Wales in this white cotton jacquard dress. Designed by Benny Ong, this button through dress is a pretty variation on the shirt dress. It was one of the more casual styles that the Princess wore on her Royal tour. According to Benny Ong, the Princess has a very positive view of her clothes. She neither needs to, nor feels she has to, dress in clothes that are different from those of other women. 'If that is what she likes and it suits her, it need not be a special design.' He is not the only person who admires this attitude. Diana's accessories on this occasion also struck exactly the right note—a white leather cummerbund belt, a shoulder bag and low-heeled pumps. A lesson in practical, stylish and charming dressing.

Adapting the style

Three piece summer suits and co-ordinates are often ideal for warmer weather. You can peel off the layers as it gets hotter. These outfits can be strikingly pretty. A good example is the beautiful printed jacket, matching skirt and contrasting plain blue camisole that the Princess first wore on her honeymoon. Designed by Donald Campbell and made in silk crêpe-de-chine, it is the sort of thing you could wear for day or evening, in town or on holiday. This style—with the soft front-tieing jacket, skirt and camisole—works best in a light-weight fabric like silk, cotton, very lightweight wool or even jersey rather than a stiff fabric. Here are some guidelines on dressing to suit your shape.

Short-waisted. Because you need to take the eye away from your high waistline, a soft front-tieing jacket needs to by-pass the waist and fall further down on the hips. Make a feature of the jacket by choosing a print that co-ordinates with a plain skirt and top. A slimmer-shaped skirt that is just slightly gathered works well with this style of jacket. Don't wear a skirt that is too short with this longer jacket as it can unbalance your look and make you seem top heavy. For the top, choose a simple camisole in a colour that coordinates with both the patterned jacket and the plain skirt.

"Splashy" print jacket...

jacket tied at hipline

wrapover jacket

batwing

printed skirt...

54

soft jacket

waistline tie

asymmetric shoulder tie

cropped jacket

Top heavy. A wrapover jacket that softly drapes across the top of the body works well, providing it is in a light-weight fabric that doesn't cling. A slightly asymmetric line of fastening can flatter a big bust. Choose a plain fabric for the jacket and team it with a printed skirt, or have them both in matching colours and fabrics. Don't go for a printed jacket with a plain skirt as this mix emphasises the bustline. A vest-shape top or one that is sleeveless rather than a strappy camisole might well be a better style for your shape. The colour of the top could be a shade darker or lighter than the jacket to give a toning effect. Keep the sleeve shape simple, like a batwing, and steer away from big puffy sleeves that end at the elbow.

Hourglass. A jacket that ties into the waist is fine providing the jacket gently blouses and falls softly onto the waist-line. With your figure, you need to emphasise the waist but without making your bust or hips look bigger. Keep the outfit very simple without too much fuss. The skirt needs to be soft, as in a dirndl shape, to match the feel of the jacket. A plain fabric in a strong clear colour would be a better choice than a powerful print. The simple camisole or vest top could then be in a coordinating print. Guard against the tendency to wear the skirt too short. Knee length is right to balance this style of jacket, and your shape.

Pear shape. Because of your bigger 'bottom' half, you cannot wear a jacket that fits into the waist or fastens at this point. It will only call attention to your problem. One idea would be to reverse the shape by fastening your jacket at the shoulder, taking the emphasis away from the waist and especially the hips. A jacket like this would work on shorter, cropped, just-above-the-waist length, as well as on a longer length, to just below the hips. Keep the skirt shape soft and full, not too gathered. A patterned skirt with a plain jacket will again make your hips a focal point, so keep the jacket patterned or have both pieces in a plain matching colour. Whatever is worn under the jacket would look best with a simple round neck, as a lower neckline would look unsightly under this shape of jacket.

A holiday wardrobe

Packing for a summer holiday can be a nightmare. The case never seems large enough, and there is always a large pile of clothes that you feel you ought to take 'just in case'. The answer is to think carefully beforehand about the sort of outfits you are going to wear. Lay all the clothes you might want to take on a worktop or a bed, and go through them carefully, deciding what goes with what. Then throw out, ruthlessly, all the things that won't fit in with your chosen looks. You will be amazed at how little you really need. Here are some guidelines.

Dresses. You need two of these. One should be suitable for sightseeing or shopping—preferably not too strappy or you may find that you have been badly sunburned without realising it. The other can be a little more 'dressy', perhaps in silk or silk mix, and would be worn for rather a smart lunch, say, or for the evening.

Skirt. Choose a simple, slightly gathered cotton or cotton jersey skirt that will go with whatever t-shirts, shirts or sweaters you will be taking. It can also be worn as a cover up for a swimsuit for both day and evening.

Cotton trousers. A pair of lightweight cotton trousers can also be teamed with your tops. Choose a fairly neutral colour, like beige, white, or even khaki. Like a skirt, trousers can be worn over a swim-suit.

t-shirts. Take a selection of these, allowing you long and short sleeves and round and low neck (or back) in a variety of different colours. One longer t-shirt or tunic shirt can double up as a beach cover or as a mini dress.

Shorts. You may need two pairs; one cut very short, like running shorts, the other a bermuda. The long pair will do not only for the beach, but for sightseeing, shopping and for evenings too.

Sweater, or a sweatshirt top. The evenings can turn chilly and a simple sweater or sweatshirt, in a colour that coordinates with your other clothes, can be very useful.

56

A kanga. This large piece of material, rather like a very big square scarf, can be very versatile. It is simply wrapped around you and fastened by tieing the ends. Wear it for the beach as a cover up, or around the waist as a skirt. Try out different ways of tieing it.

Swimwear. A swimsuit for swimming and a bikini for sunbathing is a good compromise (unless that is you go somewhere where neither is required).

Accessories. Have a small selection of scarves, long and square. A good straightforward leather belt can look good with a t-shirt and shorts, or as a waist for a kanga tied dress. Keep jewellery to a minimum, and stick to costume jewellery in case of loss or theft. You shouldn't need tights, but socks can be useful if your feet tend to overheat in canvas plimsolls or pumps. Only take comfortable shoes—a smart slip-on, an open sandal and a canvas or plastic slip-on or plimsoll style. A lightweight roly-poly style bag is worth packing. You can use it on holiday for the beach, and then fill it with souvenirs or duty-free for the journey back.

For the journey

Always travel in comfortable clothes, particularly if you are flying. Aeroplanes seem to make the body swell a little—perhaps because of the food and drink that gets consumed during the flight—so anything too tight, especially on your feet, will condemn you to an uncomfortable and unpleasant journey. Even in a car, there is absolutely no point in dressing up. A nice dress or, worse, a smart suit can so easily be ruined by crumbs, smeared food and spilled drinks. The ideal clothes for long journeys are sportswear styles—trackpants with a top in a sweatshirt fabric, for example. They wont develop unsightly creases through long hours of sitting, and they are relatively cool and absorbent. It is a good idea to wear a couple of layers so that, if it gets hot, you can peel your sweatshirt off, leaving only a t-shirt underneath. Never wear anything that restricts movement. Remember, wearing clothes that make you irritable will get any holiday off to an extremely bad start.

shirt worn as a jacket

kanga belted at hipline

bermuda shorts

ankle socks and plimsoles

roly-poly bag

sandals

Summer accessories

For casual wear, summer accessories don't differ much from winter ones. The main differences are, of course, due to the climate. You don't need thick ribbed tights in the summer. The basic rule, as before, is never to overload yourself with accessories, particularly jewellery. Big earrings and beads would look ridiculous with shorts and a t-shirt. A watch is all you need. And because you may be wearing a soft and pretty dress, it doesn't follow that your accessories should be the same. Try a heavy silver bangle and matching earrings, or perhaps just pearls, before indulging in colourful flowery beads. Silk flowers in your hair may look very pretty, but they are hardly stylish or chic.

Jewellery. Coral, pearl, wood and ivory (or a man-made look-alike) are all materials that look particularly good with summer clothes. So do such more colourful stones as turquoise, onyx and amber. Jewellery with a natural feel to it (including wood) always goes well with the lightweight fabrics and simplicity of summer clothes.

Belts. Lighter colours, particularly white or cream, are best for summer, but otherwise your needs are much the same as for winter. Long scarves make good cummerbunds worn with cotton separates or dresses.

Hats. A cotton pull-on or a peaked cap can look stylish and attractive for summer wear. A trilby-style or simple small-brimmed natural straw hat is ideal for hot, sunny weather.

Scarves. Kerchiefs can be worn around the neck, or around the head as a sweatband, or they can be tied around the waist. Cotton is the best fabric for casual summer scarves. Don't wear one as a headscarf tied under the chin. Wrapping it around the head in 'fifties style can look much better.

Tights. Naturally tanned (or even fake tanned) legs definitely look best with open toed sandals, but if you have to wear tights in hot weather for some reason, then the plainer the texture the better. Natural beige or cream coloured tights always look better with light summer clothes.

Bags. Baskets and casual canvas or fabric bags can be a good alternative to suede or leather.

Shoes. Comfortable shoes are a must in hot weather. Summer is not the time to wear fine strappy sandals if you have wide feet. Choose a fairly plain pump or court shoe as well as an easy-to-wear sandal. In general, low heels are more comfortable in hot weather. A fabric flattie or a plimsoll goes well with jeans or very casual sportswear, pants or shorts. On cooler days, try canvas boots with longer, fuller skirts.

CHAPTER THREE

Special Occasions

The Princess brings a refreshing youth and stylishness to smart dressing. This caramel, cream and beige silk two piece, designed by Arabella Pollen, was ideal for a visit to Adelaide's Parks Community Centre on a warm day in April 1983

For the majority of women, looking smart is an occasional necessity; for the Princess of Wales it is more or less a way of life. Virtually every day involves some official event; opening a new hospital, visiting a new playschool, launching ships, attending official state functions, church services, important weddings or, more sombrely, funerals, and meeting heads of state both at home and abroad. The Royal engagement diary is full of appointments which would, for the rest of us, be very special occasions indeed. It is hardly surprising, therefore, that the main part of her wardrobe is made up of these smart 'special occasion' clothes.

And what an enviable wardrobe it is—what woman would not love to have one even half as extensive and fashionable? However, life is not as easy as that and, if you are a Princess, it is often very difficult. Diana has to have a large wardrobe. She would be heavily criticised if she were to appear time after time wearing the same old outfits, or similar outfits with only minor differences between them. And she could easily have played safe—many people mistake staid, rather dull, clothes for smart ones. That, however, is not the Princess's way. Still in her early twenties, a thoroughly modern women of our time, she has a natural flair for clothes and a taste for what is interesting and different. At the same time, she has had to be aware of the need for a member of the Royal Family to dress appropriately and respectfully. Striking the right balance is never easy, but the Princess, time and time again, succeeds in standing out through looking smart when so many of the others she meets do not.

Not all the Princess's experiments have been successful, as her critics have been quick to point out. But the mistakes have been few, and Diana has learned from them. She now has confidence in her clothes, she knows what she likes to wear and she knows what is appropriate. She has developed a style of dressing smartly which is suitable, satisfying and far from stuffy.

The Princess has worn many outfits that show her sense of style in dressing for special occasions, but the dress she wore in Adelaide in April 1983, during the Australian tour, is an excellent example. (See previous page). This caramel, cream and beige silk two-piece, designed by Arabella Pollen, was a perfect choice. With its simple collarless jacket, shirt-style cuffs and soft dirndl skirt, it is the type of outfit that would take you to lunch at Claridges, tea at the Ritz, or a summer wedding. The accessories kept very much to the same mood: a honey-coloured natural straw boater hat that wasn't too sophisticated, a small cream clutch bag and low-heeled matching pumps. Diana, as she so often does, injected her own strong detail—the cream soft frilled blouse which gives the suit her own individual style. Note that she wore no heavy pieces of jewellery, which could have spoiled the whole feel of this pretty outfit.

Another, more recent, outfit, which represented a new look for the Princess, was the soft grey coloured suit which she wore for one of the happier occasions of 1983, the Queen Mother's 83rd birthday. Designed by Bruce Oldfield, the outfit has a shorter slimmer skirt and a jacket with a very fitted bodice. The result is a glamorous fashion look which would be suitable for day and evening wear.

Few, if any, of us will have to dress smartly as often as the Princess of Wales, but that doesn't mean that the occasions when we do are any less important to us. All women have to face the same problem as the Princess—how to choose

Facing page; a very special occasion for the Royal Family—the Queen Mother's 83rd birthday celebrations in the summer of 1983. This slim fitting soft grey suit was designed by Bruce Oldfield.

Darker prints in lightweight fabrics can work well for more or less any smart occasion. Here, Diana visits the Royal Marsden Cancer Hospital in a bolero-style jacket with a straight skirt and a toning blouse and kerchief.

clothes that are suitable and satisfying to wear without overdressing or looking too dull. The first of these pitfalls—overdressing—is relatively easy to avoid. Most women would realise, for example, that a clinging dress with a low plunging neckline might look very eyecatching at a formal wedding, but it would hardly be appropriate. The second pitfall—looking dull—is more likely to claim victims. Donald Campbell, who has often provided outfits for Princess Diana, points out that 'most women want to look good without being too conspicuous. And what's more, this rather timid approach is encouraged by their husbands or boyfriends too'. But, as he says, it is possible to strike a happy medium. There is an art to smart dressing, and it lies in wearing clothes that you are happy in, that project your personality and that are suitable to the occasion.

The sort of smart events you attend will depend on your lifestyle. Weddings, christenings and such things as school speechdays crop up regularly in most of our lives but you (or your husband) may have a job that requires you to dress smartly more often—for meetings, lunches, cocktail parties and so on. All of these occasions are slightly different in terms of what is practical and what is suitable. In the next few pages, you will find pictures of particularly suitable 'special occasion' clothes from the Princess's wardrobe, together with some guidelines about what to wear on those occasions when you are most likely to need to look smart.

Weddings are wonderful opportunities for dressing up (but take care not to overshadow the bride). Avoid dressing totally in cream or white if this is what the bride has chosen for her dress; or, if you must choose these colours, make sure you have plenty of accessories in other colours. Bright red or soft pastel, for instance, look good with a cream outfit, and navy, jade or pink with white. Weddings are cheerful occasions, so avoid too much black which looks a little too sombre—although black offset with plenty of white can look very striking. Choose a dress or skirt with plenty of room for movement; church services often require the congregation to kneel, and tight skirts simply don't allow for this.

Two piece outfits, like the one Diana first wore to Nicholas Soames' wedding in 1981 and again as she left Australia in April 1983 at the end of the Royal tour, are ideal. Julie Fortescue, who is the other half of the David Neil partnership, points out how practical they are. 'They can look exactly like a dress if they are made in the same fabric, and they can also be worn separately—the top with a plain skirt and the skirt with a plain blouse.' Diana also wore a dress with a two-piece feel to it to the wedding of her ex-flatmate Carolyn Pride, also in 1981, this time in the style of the Chelsea Design Company and striking exactly the right cheerful note for a happy occasion like a wedding. The versatility of these outfits is an important factor when considering your wardrobe as a whole.

Choose your fabric with care. Avoid anything that is likely to crease and stay creased, particularly if it is a wedding from midday through to the evening. Try to wear a fabric that is comfortable and that won't make you too hot. (See page 24). Accessories are also important; tottering around in high heels when you are not used to them can be very uncomfortable, and carrying too large a bag always looks messy. Weddings are occasions for hats; if you wear one, make sure that it corresponds not only in colour but in style with the rest of your outfit. Don't forget that there will be others in the congregation, and that an over-large hat can block their view.

Above; a striking combination of pink and pearls for the wedding of ex-flatmate Carolyn Pride. The dress features a favourite sailor collar. Right; this soft tunic-length top and matching fine-pleated skirt, designed by Jasper Conran, would be equally appropriate for a summer wedding or a christening. The Princess wore it to the Trooping of the Colour ceremony in 1982 and again a year later in Canada.

Finally, if you are dancing on into the night, wear something versatile that will be suitable for both the wedding and the party—for example a soft, strappy dress more formally topped with a smart jacket, or a two-piece in a delicate, light-weight fabric that will look good for the day and for the evening.

Christenings are similar to weddings in many respects, but do remember that if you are going to be holding the baby you will need to wear something washable and crush-proof. Be practical. Angora, mohair, rough tweeds and stiff leathers are not the types of fabric that would be suitable. As with weddings, a two-piece outfit can be a good choice; christenings don't come up that often

Above; the Princess turns on the Christmas lights in Regent Street in London, wearing a suit designed by Bruce Oldfield, in December 1981. This style of suit is ideal for winter weddings or cocktail parties. Right; this striking combination of vertical and horizontal blue stripes, designed by Donald Campbell, was worn in Ottawa in 1983. It would look smart in any circumstances.

and two-piece outfits or coordinates allow us to get maximum mileage from our clothes. Christenings are not usually followed by wild parties, but there is often a lot of standing around. So choose smart rather than party-style clothes and fairly practical shoes with heels of a sensible height.

Cocktail parties,

and those dinner parties where you don't need full evening dress, are times when you want to be a little individual in your style. Mix and match your own stylish separates, or accompany a new dress with a distinctive choice of accessories, such as a belt or jewellery or even a scarf. Then if, by some unfortunate chance, someone else arrives wearing the same dress as you, the similarity will be a great deal less obvious. (Of course, if this does happen, and you have the confidence, you should simply compliment the other woman on her good taste).

Black is always a good stand-by colour, and the 'little black dress' idea is as useful today as it ever was. One good thing about black is that you can wear it with many different types of accessories and each time give it a completely new look. Other good colours are red, bronze, cream, and any of the 'jewel shades' like ruby, sapphire and amethyst. In general, dark or rich colours work best.

Keep the style very simple, especially if you are going to wear the same outfit to several parties, ringing the changes by swapping your accessories. A simple silk dress can be extremely useful in these circumstances. You can wear this type of dress to work and then, simply by swapping your accessories, you can go on to a cocktail party or out to supper. Like the 'little black dress', this is something you can get plenty of wear out of. But keep the look uncluttered, not only because it looks more chic but because you may well be juggling with glasses, plates, napkins and so on. Comfortable shoes or sandals are a must for cocktail parties; they are nearly always standing room only. Silk, or jersey, or even a fine wool, make ideal fabrics to wear.

Interviews

may be decidedly un-Royal, but they are occasions that a lot of people have to face. They can be quite tricky, since the clothes you wear will depend largely on the type of job you are applying for and the impression you wish to make. The right outfit for someone applying to work in a trendy boutique would be entirely wrong for the girl who is being interviewed for a job with a bank. However, some rules apply, whatever the situation. Always try to be yourself, and dress comfortably. If you are uncomfortable, you will lack confidence in your clothes and it will show. Make sure that your clothes look well cared for—cleaned and pressed—and much the same applies to the rest of you. Pay attention to detail; check, for example, that the heels on your shoes don't need to be repaired.

Looking smart does not mean looking dull, so don't automatically go for blacks and browns. A bright, lively colour combination like grey and red, or navy and jade green, can look as cheerful to a prospective employer as it can to anyone else. And try to dress to a standard that you can maintain should you get the job. A smart suit for the interview and then jeans and a t-shirt from then on won't improve your prospects. Nevertheless, it is worth taking particular care with your appearance for an interview. This is one of those occasions when your clothes talk for you, and it is important that the first impression is good.

This three-quarter length jacket and longer straight skirt, designed by Jasper Conran, is undeniably smart. Diana wore it to Shelburne in Canada, in June 1983.

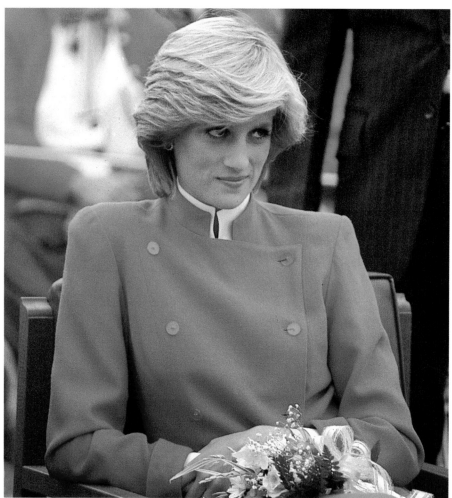

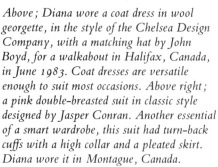

Above; Diana wore a coat dress in wool georgette, in the style of the Chelsea Design Company, with a matching hat by John Boyd, for a walkabout in Halifax, Canada, in June 1983. Coat dresses are versatile enough to suit most occasions. Above right; a pink double-breasted suit in classic style designed by Jasper Conran. Another essential of a smart wardrobe, this suit had turn-back cuffs with a high collar and a pleated skirt. Diana wore it in Montague, Canada.

Other occasions for looking smart also crop up, predictably or unpredictably, through the course of the year. Garden parties, speech days, trips to the races, shopping expeditions into town, and any of a number of semi-formal functions where we may want to create a good impression, can all call for smart, non-fussy dressing. Avoid wearing anything too bulky, like a heavy coat or a number of different layers of clothes. A suit would be ideal. You could wear it in formal style with a shirt, or, for a softer look, with a bow or tie-neck blouse. For a very 'understated' image, wear a suit with a simple silk vest or round-neck top. Dresses too look good at times like this, especially styles that are fairly tailored like shirtwaisters and coat-dresses. If you are wearing a plain dress, try throwing a patterned shawl over one shoulder. If the dress is short-sleeved, team it with a blazer or tailored jacket. Don't wear a large or complicated hat and, again, pay particular attention to detail; check your tights for snares and follow the example of some very distinguished ladies and carry a spare pair in your bag. All of this becomes twice as important if the occasion has anything to do with school. You might not mind too much what impression you create, but your children certainly do; they can be your severest critics.

Whatever the occasion, the essence of looking smart is to stand out by dressing stylishly, and not by looking garish or over-dramatic. The clever use of fabrics

Above; for the World University Games in Edmonton—a sort of grown-up international school sports day—Diana wore this slightly quilted jacket with spotted dress underneath, designed by Donald Campbell, and a toning hat. Above right; a summery outfit, in the style of the Chelsea Design Company. The Princess wore this clever combination of red and white, in plain and spot fabric, to Altona in Australia.

and colours can help a great deal in achieving this. Some people are able to wear strong distinctive clothes without feeling the least bit inhibited, and Princess Diana is one of them. Always aware of the fact that people want to pick her out in a crowd, she has to dress distinctively but not, of course, too flamboyantly. Her choice of fabrics and colours is therefore all important, sometimes more so than the actual style she wears. An excellent example of this is the silk crêpe-de-chine dress designed by Donald Campbell that she wore on both the Australian and Canadian tour (see page 70 for the design of this dress). It has a strong combination of Royal blue and white, as well as the clever mixing of two floral printed fabrics. The result is very individual and highly distinctive. Donald Campbell is a designer who loves to work with rich, colourful fabrics. 'It is a great shame' he says 'that a lot of women always think it best to play safe with colours and choose traditional soft blues, navy, camels and browns. I think it is probably because they are frightened of wearing strong colours'. As this dress shows, strong colours and mixed patterns, provided the style of the dress is kept simple, can work very well.

Donald Campbell's design is perfect for any daytime special occasion. Unfortunately, with cheaper clothes, where the fabrics and colours are not of such high quality, the mixing of two prints can go very wrong. You may find that the best way to achieve this effect is to use an accessory. A black and white floral printed dress, for instance, could be worn with a cummerbund belt in a larger or

smaller print to give a mix-and-match effect; or you could use a long printed scarf as a cummerbund in the same way. Stick to a print in the same family and follow the same colour theme.

As the Princess of Wales shows, it is worth trying to be a little adventurous in your choice of colours. Bright red, pink or blue can always be toned down a little by adding a neutral colour for accessories. Black always works well with vibrant shades. And white is ideal to wear with softer more delicate colours, as the Princess demonstrated with the white and yellow patterned silk dress designed by Jan Vanvelden, which she wore at the beginning of the Royal tour of Australia in March 1983 (see page 71 for more details). Jan Vanvelden feels strongly about accessories. 'They are extremely important as they can so easily ruin an outfit.' he says, and he always advises his clients to play them down rather than overdoing it with too many bits and pieces—particularly if they are wearing a patterned or printed dress that looks stunning anyway. The Princess's choice of a simple white leather cummerbund around the waist, white clutch bag, white court shoes, and very simple jewellery, is just right.

This dress also demonstrates how a simple shirtwaister can look cool, comfortable and entirely in place on a smart occasion. Jan Vanvelden tells us 'I think it is important for women to look relaxed in smart clothes, certainly not to be inhibited by them'. And the Princess certainly looks relaxed. Another important point about this dress is that the length is exactly right, with the soft, full skirt balancing the more detailed bodice. Skirt lengths are always a good talking point, whether it's the latest look from a catwalk show at the Paris collections, or Diana's most recent outfit. However, there is no doubt that the below-the-knee, almost mid-calf, length is right in this case. Worn as a mini, it would have looked ridiculous. You can unbalance your looks completely by wearing a skirt length that is too long or too short. Always look at your outfit as a whole. A dress with a very neat bodice, perhaps with batwing sleeves and a neck detail, would look unbalanced if the skirt were the lesser proportion of the two. Similarly, a long hip-length jacket would look absurd with a very short skirt. Balancing the lengths doesn't mean that the proportions have to be equal. A short cropped jacket looks exactly right with a longer length skirt. And different figure shapes often need different balancing. (See pages 72–75.) As with many other aspects of fashion, there are no hard and fast rules; only guidelines. But, in general, if you want to look well-dressed and smart, a slightly longer skirt length, at least to the knee, is likely to prove more elegant.

The Princess often wears printed fabrics for smart occasions, but Jan Vanvelden's dress is a particularly interesting example. The pattern is obviously one that she feels happy in since she also wears a navy and white suit in the same pattern—it is interesting to note how the same print can look entirely different in another colourway. Yellow is also often thought to be a difficult colour to wear, although, with white or cream accessories and a simple straw hat, it can look marvellous for summer weddings or christenings. Many more women would find that they could wear it if they tried.

The Princess of Wales is fortunate in that her complexion and hair colouring suit many colours besides yellow. But this shouldn't distract us from the fact that her style, even on smart and special occasions is adventurous as well as stylish. She has been as refreshing an influence on 'special occasion' clothes as she has been on other aspects of fashion. It is now much more fun to look smart than it has been for many a long year.

Diana meets local children in Charlo, Canada wearing a kimono style suit, designed by Jan Vanvelden, that incorporates many of the latest fashion pointers. It is obviously a print she likes. Earlier in the same year, she wore a silk dress in this pattern, but in white on yellow (see page 71), for a visit to Alice Springs.

This dress, with its strong colour combination of Royal blue and white, and the clever mixing of two floral print fabrics, provided the Princess with one of her most distinctive outfits. Designed by Donald Campbell, in silk crêpe-de-chine, it made its appearance in Brisbane, Australia, in April 1983 and then again in June of the same year at Alberta University, Canada. The round-necked dress has a fitted waistline with soft elbow-length sleeves, slightly padded shoulders and a gathered skirt. A matching tie belt continues the theme. Diana wore it with a minimum of accessories, and a small white tricorn shaped hat by John Boyd. Donald Campbell was very aware of the difficulties presented by a dress like this. 'Obviously' he explains 'using stronger colours like purple, red and yellow, pink and Royal blue, and mixing fabrics, only works if the style is kept simple. Never try to be too clever . . .' Putting too many colours and patterns into a dress that was already quite complex or fussy in style could end up looking a mess – something this dress triumphantly avoids.

Sunshine yellow in the softest of silk is the dress that the Princess chose to wear at the beginning of the Royal tour of Australia at Alice Springs in March 1983. Specially designed for her by Jan Vanvelden, the dress is in a simple shirtwaister style, in a distinctive abstract design, in white on yellow silk. Like all the best designers, Jan Vanvelden knows the importance of fabrics. All his prints are exclusive to the Vanvelden range, mostly bought from Italy and France, although some cottons and fine wools are from England. The style of this elegant dress incorporates several distinctive points. The winged collar neckline with the tab front button is decorated by a simple rouleau necktie with a pin-tucked front. The flattering batwing sleeve pleats gently into the top of the shoulder and the three-quarter length sleeve – slightly more formal than a short sleeve – tapers into a narrow cuff. And the soft, full skirt balances the detailed bodice. The Princess's choice of accessories for this dress – a simple white leather cummerbund, a white clutch bag and white court shoes – was exactly right.

Adapting the style

A basic tailored suit with a slim or pleated skirt is definitely a good investment buy. Even if you already have this look in your wardrobe, there may well be occasions – the wedding of a close relative or friend, for example – when you want something a bit out of the ordinary. The Princess of Wales has obviously worn plenty of different suit styles, but one that would make an interesting addition to any wardrobe is this 'jewel' green coloured two-piece in the style of the Chelsea Design Company, worn in Wellington in April 1983. It features many of Diana's favourite details. The jacket has a close fitting bodice, with a narrow stand up collar, asymmetric buttons, peplum frilled waist and a soft full skirt. A cream frilled blouse just shows above the collar. This particular suit style is not flattering for all figures, but with careful adaptation you should be able to achieve a similar look, whatever your shape.

Top heavy. A long line fitted jacket that just skims the hips is the most attractive style for this shape. Keep the jacket simple: collarless jackets are better than a mandarin style. Off-centre buttoning is good for big busted women because it takes the eye away from the centre of the bustline. Set-in sleeves are flattering, but deep frilled peplum waists are not as they tend to emphasise the top of the body and bustline too much. You could, however, wear a narrow belt to comphasise the waistline. Keep the skirt soft, possibly in a dirndl shape, and not

stand collar...
raglan sleeves....
hipline....
belted at a
slim skirt....
flat pumps....

Simple round neckline....
peplum waist....
tapering skirt....

too wide. If you choose a darker colour like black, grey or navy, try teaming it with brighter coloured accessories. Don't overdo the jewellery.

Pear shaped. Here you have the opportunity to mix printed and plain fabrics together. A printed jacket with a plain skirt would put the emphasis on the top half of the body, with flattering effect. Larger hip shapes can afford to wear a high collar with a frilled blouse underneath. The jacket can have a side closure, and full tapering sleeves. Never choose a deep peplum waist as it will fall right on the heaviest part of you. Go for a straighter-cut longer-line jacket especially if it's in a print. Keep the skirt a dirndl shape and go for unpressed pleats rather than gathers. If you are going to mix print and plain, do keep them in the same colourway, and make sure that the shades complement each other rather than clash.

Short-waisted. Peplums and short cropped jackets are not flattering. To bring the emphasis away from the waist and onto the hips, choose a slightly fuller, almost 'blouson' style, jacket that has a belt worn low on the hip. This style of jacket looks good with a simple stand-up collar and with the raglan sleeve line. If the body of the jacket is fairly full, avoid full puffed sleeves, which can make the overall appearance very fattening. A slimmer skirt shape would balance the fuller jacket. A deep, strong colour can make this smart but rather 'sporty' suit very versatile.

Hourglass. Try a '40s style suit. It will flatter your shape. A simple round-neck jacket could be fitted with deeper-cut sleeves that are not gathered into the armhole. Either centre or side fastening would do. A peplum around the waist would give the right emphasis to your waistline, but make sure that it's not too deep or it will make your hips too prominent. And for a slimmer head-to-toe silhouette, try a straight, almost tapering, skirt shape. This style of suit could be worn as a two-piece with no blouse underneath. It would then work well in a plaid or check fabric in deep rich colours. High heeled shoes look good with this style of suit.

Adapting the style

A smart classic dress is a wise addition to any wardrobe. It can be worn on many different occasions and, if the design is a simple one, you won't easily tire of it. The Princess has worn a number of classic styles, but one that has all the right stylish qualities is the soft, dusky blue, drop-waist dress with a fine pleated skirt, which she wore in Charlottetown in June 1983 during the Royal tour of Canada. Designed by Jan Vanvelden in wool crêpe the dress is almost tailored in style, but softened by the delicate scalloped sailor collar. This, and indeed any other, style of dress can be adapted to suit different types of figure.

Top heavy. Choose simple necklines with no big frills or ruffles, and steer clear of high collars and fussy bodice detail. A simple, very slightly scooped, slashed neckline with a narrow trim would be good. This trim detail could then be picked out around the drop-waist seam, bringing the focal point away from the bust. Keep arm-holes and sleeve detail simple – full,

white trim on slash neck

pleated collar

tucked sleevehead

fitted bodice

pleats

pleats from hipline

printed skirt

full skirt

light legs

black piping bow

pleats from hipline

contrast shoes

tucked sleevehead

fitted to hipline

full pleated skirt from hipline

tinted legs

elbow-length sleeves will make you look even more top heavy. A colourful, simple print would give the dress a classic feel, but keep away from horizontal stripes and fluffy or clinging fabrics, particularly over the bustline.

Pear shape. A style that shows off your waist will remove the emphasis from your hips much more effectively than a drop waist. Go for strong bodice detail – frills, ruffles or a beautiful white pleated collar with perhaps a small bow trim. Elbow-length sleeves carefully tucked on the shoulder to give a gentle 'puff' shape are a good detail. Keep your skirt full but not heavily gathered and avoid sunray pleats and big patch pockets.

Short-waisted. A drop-waist dress (or one that doesn't have any waist at all) is perfect for your shape. Be bold in your choice of colour and detail. A bright Royal blue with a contrasting white collar, piped in black, and a matching bow can look stunning. Soft pleats are a good choice for the skirt, providing they don't start at the waist.

Hourglass. A figure skimming style of dress will show off your curves to best effect. You can afford to wear a dress that has a pretty collar feature, providing it is not too bold or overpowering. For a looser shaped dress, like a drop waist, to be flattering, you need to add a belt or sash to call attention to your waistline. Make the belt your main accessory detail. Go for a sleeve shape that's full at the top and then tapers into the wrist, and a soft, slightly fuller, skirt, which can be gently pleated. Because you can wear a style of dress that is fairly busy, a plain fabric would probably be best. Steer clear of clinging fabrics like jersey or fine knits. A lightweight wool crêpe or silk would be most flattering.

The Princess looks respectfully sombre at the Remembrance Day parade in November 1981. Nevertheless, the white frilled collar is a distinctive and very characteristic touch.

Gilt-edged investments

Nobody with any sense would grudge the Princess of Wales her large and varied wardrobe, particularly when she has done so much for the image of British fashion, both at home and abroad. And who, anyway, would want the future Queen of England to look dull and dowdy? However, her wardrobe may not be as large as many people think. Many of the outfits she wears are not new at all; they are things that she has worn before, but which she has cleverly adapted to give them a completely new look.

This is the value of investment buying, the knack of choosing classic clothes that can be adapted for different occasions and worn over and over again. Adapting your clothes and giving them a fashion update is the way in which most well-dressed women control their wardrobes. With clothes becoming more and more costly, nobody can afford to fritter away money on senseless outfits.

The collar is familiar, but there the similarities end. The blouse is the same as the one on the opposite page, but here it is used to transform Donald Campbell's printed silk dress on a visit to Chesterfield.

Rather than dashing out and buying a complete new look each season, stylish and sensible women add to and update their existing wardrobes.

There are many examples of Diana's use of 'investment dressing'. For example, she wore a black suit and white satin blouse designed by Bellville Sassoon for the Remembrance Sunday ceremony in November 1981. Taking the same blouse, she uses it to give a new look to the red, black and white printed dress by Donald Campbell that she wore on a subsequent visit to Chesterfield. The collar detail is a dominant feature on both occasions. At Ascot in 1981, the Princess wore several different outfits. One of them was a silk 'pyjama' stripe three-piece, designed by David Neil, in banana, fuschia and Royal blue (see next page for further details). In Holbrook, during the Royal tour of Australia, in 1983, we saw Diana in the same outfit. This time, she had changed the style, now wearing it as a two-piece with a small bow detail tied at the neck. A change of accessories, picking out the fuschia colour for the small pill-box hat, designed by John Boyd,

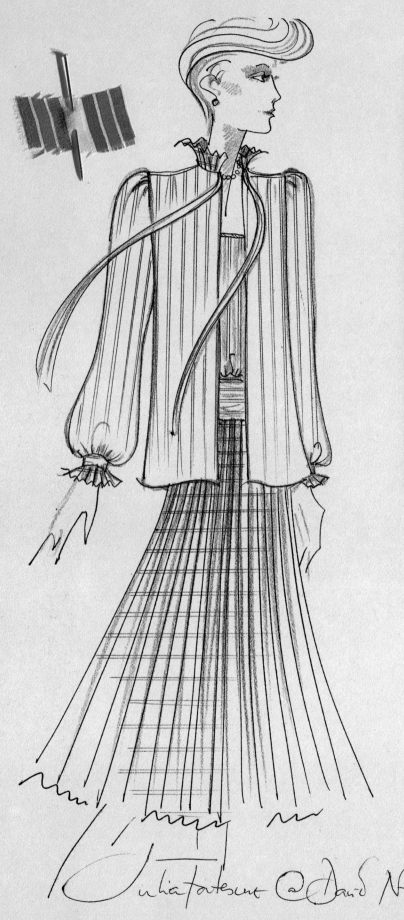

The Princess obviously numbers this outfit among her favourites. First worn to Ascot in the summer of 1981, it reappeared with different accessories in Australia two years later—demonstrating the versatility of these elegant suits. The three pieces making up the outfit are a camisole, a blouse with a soft frilled collar that could be worn inside or outside, and a matching soft pleated skirt. Made in silk crêpe-de-chine, in striking narrow banana, fuschia and Royal blue stripes, the overall effect is cheerful and refreshing. The designers, David Bates and Julie Fortescue, who make up the David Neil label, have created several of these outfits. This one, David Bates explains, was part of their collection in 1981. It caught the Princess's discerning eye, and so they made it up for her in a different fabric. It wouldn't do for the Princess to coincide with someone else who might have bought it.

and adopting a smart 'gucci' style printed clutch bag and plain black court shoes, completed the transformation; a new look from old!

There are plenty of other examples. In Canberra in 1983 she wore the peach silk dress and jacket by Belville Sassoon that she first wore on her wedding day as her going away outfit. In fact, two versions of the jacket were made, one with short sleeves and one with long because, as David Sassoon points out 'you can never be sure of the weather'. Fortunately the weather was perfect on the wedding day, so the short-sleeved jacket was worn on that occasion. Another example was the outfit the Princess wore for Prince William's christening in November 1982 which appeared again in Sydney in April 1983. And there are many more. They all demonstrate the fact that investment clothes are part of even the most fashionable wardrobe.

Right; the outfit the Princess wore for Prince William's christening reappears in Sydney, Australia, this time with a different coloured hat and accessories.

Clever collars

One of the best ways of giving a plain dress or suit a new look is to add a new collar. This need not involve advanced dressmaking skills, just a little initiative and imagination. Princess Diana often uses collars as a way of giving an outfit a new look, or of giving it a touch of distinction. Her much loved frills, especially a pierrot collar on a soft blouse, are famous. They give, for example, an entirely different feel to Jasper Conran's tailored white collarless jacket and skirt suit. If you don't have a blouse that can give this effect, try tieing a piece of lace around the neck or buy a separate lace collar. These will add a pretty touch to slightly more 'masculine' tailored clothes. It is worth searching the bric-a-brac shops and markets for antique lace, since it also goes well with heavy tweeds and velvet. Sailor collars are another favourite, as on her Chelsea Design style outfit (see page 63), and also on many of her maternity outfits. Here again, you could use a piece of lace, or a long plain scarf to achieve a similar effect.

Not many collars are as distinctive as the large, Van Dyke style, scalloped collar that Jan Vanvelden has used on several of the suits and dresses he has designed for the Princess. But it shows that a bold contrasting collar can be very effective. Detachable collars are not often thought of as accessories, but they are quite widely available and they can make a lot of difference to the versatility of your wardrobe.

Hats make headlines

Above; a blue tricorn hat with specially dyed veil and feather trim at the back. Diana first wore this when her pregnancy was announced. Here she is in Wrexham.

Right; the Princess shows the effectiveness of dressing in a single colour throughout. With Jasper Conran's cream suit, on a visit to Launceston, Tasmania, she wears a tiny cream silk hat with matching veil and silk flower trim.

One of the more enduring of the Princess's trademarks has been her hats. They were an early part of her distinctive style of dress, and have remained so ever since. This has had a noticeable effect on fashion generally. No longer are hats solely the adornment of middle-aged women on rather pompous occasions; they are part of the wardrobe of almost all fashion-conscious young women.

Diana's styles in hats vary enormously. It seems that, whatever her outfit, she has a hat to suit it. However, there are one or two that appear to be favoured above the rest. As John Boyd, her favourite milliner, says, 'The Princess likes wearing hats, particularly the small veiled ones.' In fact, it is said that her fondness for this style dates back to the first time she wore it, at the Trooping of the Colour in 1981. Prince Charles is supposed to have commented on how pretty it looked, and from then on, it has reappeared with great regularity.

A hat is a very important accessory, but it is one that it is often quite difficult to judge. As John Boyd explains, 'Most women look ahead, straight into the mirror, when trying on a hat, when really they should turn to look at their profile to see how the hat suits them from this important angle.' This is well worth

remembering—as Diana seems to do. Apparently, she knows as soon as she puts on a hat whether it suits her or not. Obviously, you should choose a hat that suits you, the occasion and the rest of your clothes. But don't always go for the obvious style. It doesn't necessarily follow that a large hat will suit a large lady. Bone structure is more important than body shape. And don't go for a hat with too many trims. The right combination such as a veil and a pom, can look delightful on the right shape of hat, and disastrous on the wrong one.

Hats, unlike many other items of clothing, do not last for ages. The phrase 'old hat' has some substance to it. Nothing looks as sad as an old hat. Look after your hats well, but don't expect them to go on for years.

Above; another matching hat is this satin pill-box hat with a large pom trim and a tiny jewel detail. Diana correctly wears it slightly tipped to the right, following the natural flow of the body.

Above; Diana wears a larger-brimmed off-white 'Pari' straw hat with Jan Vanvelden's navy and white suit for a visit to Auckland in April 1983. Right; the 'Breton' is another style that the Princess has worn several times. Often worn on the back of the head (remember to check your profile to see if it suits you), the Princess wears it slightly more forward. A small velvet bow trim worn at the side is discreetly tucked under the brim. Diana wore this on a visit to Liverpool to open a Chinese Community Centre. Far right; this large, floppy 'artist's' beret in suede, designed by Steven Jones, is one of the few of Diana's hats to have been designed by another milliner. This can be a difficult style to wear, but here, in Liverpool, with an outfit by Arabella Pollen, Diana succeeds with her usual ease.

Building on your basic wardrobe

The basic wardrobe described in Chapter One (see page 20) will carry you through quite a lot of occasions but there are bound to be times when you want to look particularly smart. For these 'special occasions' you need to add to and adapt your basic wardrobe. Here are some suggestions as to how to go about it.

The two most useful additions you can make to your wardrobe are a simple silk elasticated-waist style dress, and a two-piece blazer-style suit. The classic silk dress is ideal for any special occasion. In plain black with lots of pearls, it would steal the show at any cocktail party; in a sophisticated smart print, like a Prince of Wales check, it would look suitably elegant for an interview or a school speech day. Try adding a large shawl or scarf in a contrasting colour for a more stylish look. Don't forget to colour coordinate your tights and shoes (and indeed the rest of your accessories). A soft leather cummerbund belt makes an excellent waistline feature.

A simple blazer suit is probably the most versatile outfit you can buy, capable of being adapted for almost any occasion. There has recently been a strong swing in fashion to more tailored styles, which are fairly sophisticated and yet comfortable to wear. These tailored jackets lend themselves to an endless variety of uses. They go well with either full or straight skirts provided they are not too heavy or tweedy, and look equally good with dresses. They can turn a smart pair of trousers into a trouser suit. They can be dressed up with a frilled blouse, or a big bow tied at the neck, making them ideal for weddings and christenings. They can be worn in a more 'understated' style, with a silk t-shirt top or vest, to give a more sophisticated look that would suit a cocktail party or a special dinner date. A little extra touch for stylish dressing would be provided by a silk handkerchief in the top pocket. A shirt with a small collar looks good with the collar turned up; and wide velvet or tartan ribbons, tied in a bow and worn under a collar, can be a very attractive accessory feature.

Never underestimate the value of a good blazer suit. If you buy one that is well made, it will last for years.

classic dress in a sophisticated smart print

contrasting scarf

large bow neckline on shirt

simple blazer suit

Colour co-ordinated tights & shoes

Royal accessories

The way the Princess uses accessories is a major part of her 'special occasion' style. The keynote again is simplicity. If she is wearing a high-neck frilled blouse, she doesn't add long earrings and a variety of necklaces. A single piece of daytime jewellery is all that is necessary. Many women panic when faced with a special occasion. Everything available—a hat, earrings, chains, rings and bracelets, and heavy shoulder bag—is thrown on in a way that might work for a Christmas tree, but not for someone trying to look smart. Even the combination of earrings, necklace and a brooch looks clumsy and old fashioned. Here, as elsewhere, the Princess shows definite taste. The choker style necklace, especially in pearls, is a familiar choice. Her influence can be seen in the costume jewellery market, as styles once reserved for evening wear are now worn during the daytime as well. Diamante earrings can look very good with a formal suit, as can plenty of pearls.

Her choice of handbags shows a similar taste. Gone are the rather clumsy, old fashioned and typically 'Royal' handbags that had to be carried around cumbrously on the arm. In their place, she chooses a small neat clutch or occasionally shoulder bag in colours that coordinate with the rest of her outfit. Her shoes, too are kept simple. She rarely goes for fancy trims, strappy sandals or high heels, and wears instead the famous 'Diana' low-heeled court shoes, which go so well with both suits and dresses. Again, she often coordinates her shoe colour with the rest of her outfit, or successfully combines accessories in a dark colour like black with a light coloured outfit. Almost any photograph of the Princess demonstrates her stylish use of accessories, but the one on the left sums them all up. With Donald Campbell's spotted and striped dress, in Auckland in 1983, she wore only pearl earrings, necklace and small clutch bag; an elegant and uncluttered look.

Accessory checklist

Just as different types of occasions demand different types of clothes, so too do they demand different accessories. A basket won't look good with a smart suit, and nor are trainers the best footwear to go with a sophisticated dress. This may seem obvious, but if you are splashing out and buying fairly expensive clothes, it seems silly to ruin your looks by choosing the wrong accessories. Here is a check list of accessories that will be suitable for 'special occasions'.

Jewellery. When you want to look smart, rely on one or two distinctive pieces of jewellery. Never wear too much. If you can't afford the genuine article, good fake costume jewellery is well worth buying. Try mixing not-so-obvious styles of jewellery with classic clothes. For example, a big glass 'jewel' brooch looks very stylish on a tweed jacket; and two or three rows of pearls on a simple, plain wool dress can look

marvellous. In the same way, you may need only a fairly large pair of drop earrings to set off a smart suit. Don't make the mistake of wearing gold and silver together; a silver bracelet and gold earrings are much better worn separately. As with all accessories, use jewellery ro ring the changes on your classic investment clothes, and to inject a sense of fun and new fashion trends.

Belts. Two or three good leather belts are a vital accessory for a smart wardrobe—a soft leather cummerbund, a narrower belt and a classic, heavier, leather belt. Keep the buckles simple. A light and a dark colour are best for all-round use, but a fashion colour for a belt could make a well worn suit look refreshingly different.

Scarves. Colourful, plain scarves are probably more use than anything too heavily patterned, although a patterned scarf worn cleverly around the neck can very effectively alter the appearance of simple, plain dress. Similarly, a shawl or

long wool scarf can look great with an elegant suit. Experiment with scarves to find out what suits you best.

Tights. Patterned tights, if they are not too bold, and coloured tights that match your skirt are often better than natural colours. A ribbed or 'feathery' texture goes well with country fabrics like tweeds and herring-bones. Use tights to alter the look of a simple outfit.

Bags. Either clutch or shoulder style. Steer away from 'handbags' that you need to carry on your arm.

Shoes. The shoes in your basic wardrobe should see you through. If you have the money, extend the range of colours and styles.

Hats. Depending on your outfit and your hairstyle there are two good basic hat-shapes that seem to suit most occasions; the smaller pillbox style, and the larger wide-brimmed felt or straw hat. (See page 81.)

CHAPTER FOUR

Evening Wear

It is in her evening wear that Diana most lives up to the image of a fairy Princess. Here, she dances with the Prince of Wales at a formal dinner and dance at Government House in Canberra, Australia, in March 1983. This drop-waist style, slim-fitting ballgown, with leg-of-mutton sleeves, was designed by Murray Arbeid and made in pale yellow silk taffeta.

F airy-tale floating organza ballgowns; sharp-coloured rustling taffetas; clothes that belong to the film screen or even only to our dreams; these, above all else are what we associate with the Princess of Wales. Here is style at its purest. Whether she is wearing a traditional ballgown or an eyebrow-raising slinky evening dress, she never looks less than perfect, and never fails to delight her audience. She has the style of a true Princess. Formal evening dress is part of the uniform of the British Royal family. State banquets, film premieres, Royal Command Performances, all demand full evening dress. In the past these events have called for a style of dressing that was rather staid and definitely predictable. There have been some beautiful gowns, but nobody would have described them as fashionable or chic. Thanks to Princess Diana, that has all changed. Since those early days, of the strapless black taffeta evening dress, the Princess has brought glamour, sophistication and fantasy to evening wear. And where better to do it? On what other occasions do we need to think only of looking like a Princess ourselves—radiant, happy and beautiful? The answer, of course is none.

The Princess has worn dresses that cover the whole gamut of evening styles. And, although most women will never own a Bellville Sassoon or a Bruce Old-field evening gown, their influence can be seen at every formal evening function across the country. This has had the effect of making almost any evening occasion an opportunity for stylish and fashionable dressing. Whether the occasion is a dinner dance, or an evening at the opera, a ball or a select dinner party, or something less formal like a party or a visit to a discotheque, there are exciting clothes to wear. In fact, the difficulty usually lies in deciding how formal you should be. It would be a bit much to wear a ballgown to a discotheque. Choosing what to wear can often be harrowing if you don't know exactly what is expected of you. But things are easier now than they used to be. At one time, only full-length dresses could be worn for formal occasions. Today, this isn't so. The new, shorter evening dresses are becoming increasingly popular, and they are, of course, much more versatile than the traditional ballgown so that they can be worn to all but the most formal evening occasions, from dinners and parties to dances and the theatre. Accessories, too, have become more flexible. Evening gloves were once *de rigeur* for evening dress. Today, they are no longer necessary.

There are still occasions, however, when you have to dress up. You may have been asked to a very formal dinner and dance, or a rather grand anniversary. Or you may have received an invitation bearing the words 'Dress: formal' or 'Black Tie', when the men will have to wear formal evening dress suits and the women will have to dress to the same standard. These are marvellous opportunities to escape from the ordinary, more practical, clothes that you wear every day. They are chances to have fun. The problem here is to choose something that is striking without being outrageous, and suitable without being dull.

As in all other aspects of dressing with style, the keynotes are suitability, practicality and simplicity. Almost all the Princess of Wales' evening outfits demonstrate an awareness of these rules, none more so perhaps than the shimmering ballgown she wore to the ballet in Auckland New Zealand in April 1983. Designed by Donald Campbell, in lilac silk taffeta, it demonstrates how a simple off-the-shoulder dress, in a single colour, can look entirely appropriate and

Facing page; the off-the-shoulder style is one of the Princess's favourites. This dress, in lilac silk taffeta, was designed by Donald Campbell and worn to the ballet in Auckland, New Zealand in April 1983.

entirely stunning. And the pale yellow ballgown she wore to a formal dinner and dance at Government House, Canberra, in March 1983, (see page 85) showed off her figure in a way that needed no further emphasis.

It requires confidence to wear flamboyant clothes—there is no point in wearing a strapless evening dress if you are going to spend the whole evening with your shoulders hunched wishing you hadn't. It is worth remembering that a bare back or shoulder can have as much, if not more, sex-appeal as a large expanse of cleavage. And you can sit, chat, dance, and eat comfortably throughout the evening without worrying about what you might be revealing.

Evening wear can be expensive, particularly the more formal styles, and you are unlikely to get as much mileage out of them as you do from your daytime clothes. Nevertheless, following in the Princess of Wales' footsteps, many manufacturers have adapted her styles and made them available at much more affordable prices. The top designers, whose clothes appear throughout this book, nearly all design ready-to-wear ranges of clothes, including evening wear, which are available from top stores and shops throughout the country. It is unlikely, however, if not impossible, that you could buy exactly the same dress as the Princess. While she may often choose a style from the designer's range, she will have it adapted to suit her own individual taste. (See page 95 for an example). This certainly doesn't mean that she has all her evening dresses specially designed for her. The beautiful deep-shaded tartan taffeta she wore to the premiere of *E.T.* was an off-the-peg dress designed by Roland Klein and bought in Bond Street.

Despite the lure of the fabulous dresses in the big city stores, you can sometimes be better off in a smaller shop where they will take the time to give you a much more personal service. There is an added advantage in this: if you are buying something special for a local occasion, a smaller shop will be able to tell you whether somebody else who might be going has bought the same dress. They will also be readier, and quicker, to carry out any alterations that you might want. You don't have to be the Princess of Wales to prefer not to turn up wearing the same dress as someone else.

Almost any colour seems to suit Princess Diana, and, as with her other clothes, she has worn a wide range of them at different times. The only exception is black, in which she is only rarely seen—the Royal Family tend to reserve black for mourning. Paradoxically, black is one of the commonest colours for evening wear generally, whereas white or cream, or very pale colours, which the Princess wears so well, are fairly unorthodox. The delightful ball gown designed by Gina Fratini (see page 92), and the frothy sequined dress designed by David and Elizabeth Emanuel are examples of the very effective use of these relatively uncommon colours. If nothing else, these outfits demonstrate that there is no need to restrict yourself to conventional colours when choosing your evening wear. There are more colours in the dress designers palette than black, red, blue and pink.

The colour that you choose for your own evening wear is very much a matter of individual choice. It depends on your skin and hair colouring (see page 18) as well as on your personality. But again there are points worth bearing in mind. If the style is rather complicated, with lots of frills, bows and pleats, you will find that it looks much better if you stick to a plain or very delicately patterned fabric. Contrasting colours can also work well. Black with gold or silver can be extremely effective. But very few women can wear all-gold or all-silver outfits with success unless the style is kept very simple. If you want to see how it is done, have another look at the amazing one-shoulder, body skimming dress, with an

Above left; Diana celebrates her new found slimness at the priemiere of E.T. *in this off-the-peg strapless evening dress, in a marvellous mixture of velvet and taffeta, designed by Roland Klein. Above right; very pale colours, like white, are not often worn for evenings, but this beautiful sequined gown, by David and Elizabeth Emanuel, which the Princess wore to the Welsh National Opera in Cardiff, and also for a state banquet for the king of Saudi Arabia, shows just how effective they can be.*

exquisite mixture of cream and silver beads, that Princess Diana wore in Australia and at the premiere of *Octopussy* (see pages 12 and 98). Here is simplicity used with maximum impact.

Of course, this dress succeeds not only because of its simplicity of style, but also because of the fabric. Alas, it is almost impossible to capture this sort of look from a fabric that is very much cheaper. Copies are rarely made using the same fabric anyway. Beautiful fabrics, like delicate hand-painted chiffon, encrusted with sequins or beads, are difficult, if not impossible, to reproduce cheaply. You will, however, find some acceptable imitations in chiffon taffetas, moire, lace, satin, jersey and crêpes. But always remember that the fabric must suit the style of the dress. A silk jersey type of fabric, which gives and stretches, looks best for a body skimming style, but it won't work for a fuller, more conventional style of ballgown. For this, you will be much better off with taffeta or silk chiffon. The brst way to judge a dress is by the quality of the fabric. Don't be taken in by the spurious charms of clothes that are made of inferior fabrics but which may look more glamorous. They never look better in the end.

A birthday dress for a Princess. Both it and its wearer survived a damp occasion unruffled. Designed by Jan Vanvelden, the bold regal red and the matching lace top give this dress great distinction. It was worn for a farewell banquet at Government House in Edmonton, Canada.

Princess Diana's style of evening dress shows ingenuity in other ways as well. She has, for example, mixed different fabrics together with great success. Her red lace and Duchesse satin dress, designed by Jan Vanvelden, has a fitted bodice and narrow straps with a simple lace top that enhances rather than hides the dress. She has also (perhaps unintentionally) found an unusual solution to the hemline problem. Hemlines rise and fall with the changing tides of fashion and, although formal evening wear is usually long—or ankle length—it has occasionally risen to mid-calf or ballerina length. This is not an easy length to wear and tends to be more flattering to younger women. The peacock blue silk evening dress, designed for the Princess by Bruce Oldfield, neatly overcomes uncertainties about hemline length by combining short and long. Starting at knee length on one side, it falls to the floor on the other. This, combined with the deep off-the-shoulder ruffles and drop waist with a big bow at the hip, gives the dress a slight feel of the 1920s and makes it both elegant and distinctive.

Princess Diana's attitude to evening wear is clearly one that we could all adopt: if you are going to dress up, do it properly with style and panache. Above all, enjoy yourself.

One of the more daring of Princess Diana's evening gowns. This dress, by Bruce Oldfield, with its one-shoulder design and hitched hemline, caused some excitement. Some of the more old fashioned critics thought it too unorthodox for a Princess; but most people welcomed it and saw it as further evidence of the Princess's sense of style, and awareness of fashion. The dress has been worn several times, but she is seen here at a charity fashion show at the Guildhall in November 1982.

cream silk
chintz

cream
satin
baby ribbon
slotting
+ bows

organza
+ lace
Petties
organza
+ lace sleeves

'My brief was to design a dress that was formal,' explains Gina Fratini, who designed this beautiful cream-coloured ballgown, it was to be worn at the Royal couple's farewell banquet at the Sheraton Hotel in Auckland at the end of the New Zealand tour. The main part of the dress is made in organza and lace trim, with matching underskirts to give it its wonderful full shape. The bodice and the sleeves bear the main features of the dress; the pin-tucked bodice is topped by a scooped neckline with a tiny frilled trim, and the translucent elbow-length sleeves are trimmed with satin and lace with fine baby ribbon thread and bows. The dress is a fine example of how the right amount of detail, used simply and harmoniously, can have the most striking effect.

Gina Fratini
'83

This was the ballgown that did more than anything else to transform Princess Diana into a fairy-tale Princess. Designed by Bellville Sassoon, the dress is all that a ballgown should be and a bit more besides. The delicate silk chiffon fabric gives it a dreamy, romantic effect, and enhances the Princess's skin and hair colouring to perfection. And the off-the-shoulder neckline adds a touch of genuine glamour. See how attractive a bare shoulder can look! Diana first wore this to the Splendours of the Gonzago Exhibition at the Victoria and Albert Museum in November 1981, and has since worn it on several other occasions, including the premiere of Ghandi. The pattern is light and airy, with soft whispers of colour in pink and blue on white, and with tiny silver glittering specks scattered all over it. As David Sassoon says, 'Fabrics are all important for this type of dress; anything too heavy would be too harsh and ruin the rather soft, floaty effect.' The dress has all the Princess's favourite details, but here they have been transformed into new and original ideas. The neckline frill has been adapted to form the bodice and the sleeves, and this frill is then repeated in a narrower width around the hem of the skirt. Tiny bows and a sash belt provide the finishing touches.

Blue + Silver
Silk Georgette
Cascades of frills
from shoulder to
hem - Floating
skirt panel,
cinched waist of
metallic blue leather

Bruce Oldfield.

Another of the Princess's dream dresses was
this beautiful blue evening gown, designed by
Bruce Oldfield and worn to a charity ball at
the Wentworth Hotel in Sydney during the
Australian tour. This short-sleeved style,
made in bright blue silk chiffon laced through
with shimmering silver thread, cleverly
incorporates Princess Diana's favourite frilled
trim, but achieves a highly original effect by
positioning it on the sleeves and at the side of
the dress. The dress seems to float effortlessly
in space. The stylish use of silver for
accessories, especially the wide cummerbund
belt, gives this outfit a strong and vibrant
look. Worn again in New Brunswick in
Canada, it remains a favourite of the
Princess's many admirers.

The Princess's love of bright colours is sometimes reflected in her evening wear, and pink seems to be one of her favourites. This evening dress was designed by Victor Edelstein and features the drop waistline that Diana often adopts for her daytime wear. The original design shown here was slightly adapted for the Princess, as Victor Edelstein explains. The narrow petticoat straps were added, as were the big floppy bows on the shoulders—probably as a concession to sheer practicality rather than for reasons of suitability. Strapless dresses can be difficult to wear and have been known to move. The Princess cannot afford to take chances, even at the private reception given for her and the Prince of Wales by Pierre Trudeau in Ottawa in June 1983, where she first wore this dress. The shape of this dress is much slimmer than that of many of her other ballgowns, and it shows off her superb figure to perfection. The choice of fabric is very important to complement the style—silk chiffon gives it a very light feeling that prevents the dress from appearing too stiff, and works well for the tucked details which are used on the bodice and around the bottom part of the full skirt. This is a dress that proves the point that simplicity can be stunning.

Victor Edelstein

Dressing to suit your shape.

More mistakes are made with evening wear than with any other type of dress. Women are often uncertain about what suits them best, and find it hard to identify their particular figure problems. We all have fantasies about ourselves, particularly when it comes to glamorous clothes like evening gowns. We may like to think of ourselves wearing slinky dresses with plunging necklines and thigh-high splits in the side, the undoubted main attraction of the ball. But if the sad truth is that you are overweight and 4ft 11 in tall, you had better think again. Almost every dress can be adapted in more or less subtle ways to minimise your shortcomings and to make the most of your good points. And using your common sense when buying a dress will pay handsome dividends. Wearing clothes that flatter you will give you extra confidence, and you will wear them with style.

One of the most popular of formal evening styles is the rather full-skirted ballgown in delicate and pretty fabrics. A good example of this sort of look is the beautiful pink and gold dress designed by the Chelsea Design Company and worn by the Princess in April 1983 in Melbourne Australia. How can you achieve a look as good as this if your figure is rather less ideal than the Princess's? Here are some suggestions.

Pear shape. You need to remove the emphasis from your hips, so do not go for peplum or frill detail around the waist or hips. Have the main detail in the top half of your dress to balance the bigger hip shape. For instance, a soft ruffle around a slightly low v-neck and large elbow-length puff sleeves are some of the right sort of details. Don't wear a drop waist, and if you are going to wear a sash, then wear it at the waistline, never on the hips. Emphasising your waist need not make your hips look bigger, but don't wear anything too tight. A soft full skirt is the ideal shape, and you can always splash out by

choosing a strong bright colour and following the theme through in the rest of your outfit. Keep your jewellery to a single style. Large earrings with a matching 'finer' necklace would be ideal.

Top heavy. A strapless dress is not the most flattering shape for big-busted women to wear. On the other hand, high, fussy neck lines are not going to be very complimentary either. You need to strike a happy medium, for example with a fairly generous v-neck (not a plunge) with perhaps a frill that folds onto the neckline to soften the look. Remember, a generous bust needs subtle

puff sleeves...

off the shoulder...

soft ruffle neckline...

deep cummerbund...

drop waistline with peplum...

tapering sleeves...

rather than obvious emphasis. Again, a fitted shaped bodice is the most flattering. If you wanted to, you could afford to wear a peplum waistline, with soft narrow frills at the cuffs to match. This small, fluted trim could then be repeated at the hem of the skirt. Never choose too clinging a fabric for this style of dress.

Keep your jewellery fairly simple. A single bold piece, for example long pear-shaped gem earrings, or diamante drop earrings, would not be too big and would look good with no necklace at all. Alternatively, tiny pearl stud earrings with a pearl choker could be very effective.

Hourglass. Ballgowns and traditional evening dresses are very flattering to this shape. Always make sure that you have a definite waistline; this, together with a fine elasticated neckline, will show you at your best. A deep sash or cummerbund is ideal, and can even be tied in a bow to give a touch of extra femininity. Otherwise, a pretty off-the-shoulder dress with a soft frill trim that can be repeated around puff-shaped sleeves, would give just the right amount of detail. The off-the-shoulder line would be more attractive than a too deep neckline. Choose a style in a lightweight fabric that moves with you as you walk.

Short-waisted. The drop-waist evening dress was made for you—anything waisted never seems to fit you properly. The simple lines of a drop-waist evening dress can be made more romantic by adding a soft ruffle that lies not too high around the neck. Follow this detail through with a peplum on the low waistline and at the end of full tapering sleeves. Interesting earrings would work well with this neckline. A drop shape in pearl and diamante or crystal is all that would be needed. Remember, the more complicated the style, the more you should beware of busy patterns or too many details like ribbons and lace.

Adapting the style

If you find ballgowns and traditional evening dresses rather demure for your taste, and want something with a bit more glamour to it, you probably adored the one-shoulder evening dress that the Princess has worn with such success. It is not easy to wear this look unless you are fairly evenly proportioned; but there are certain ways of adapting this rather figure-hugging style to give a similar slimmer appearance to other, different, figure shapes. One way, for example, is to go for a striking colour like black, which works particularly well with the more shape-revealing styles. Brighten up black by choosing different coloured accessories. Silver and gold look marvellous for shoes and bags; (they are often chosen by the Princess). For jewellery, bold costume styles in an array of colours and materials, from diamante to pearl and from coloured glass to gilt, always look good on black. Or, on a plain black dress, a tiny diamante trim around a simple neckline can look great.

Pear shape. There is no way of making a style that is too body-hugging look good on someone with big hips. At the other extreme, a large 'sack' shape will only make you look frumpy and bigger. The best way to get over the problem is to go for a striking top half that will combine well with a softer skirt to give you an overall slimmer appearance. The one-shoulder look is fine, provided that the top is fairly fitted and blends in with the soft skirt shape. Steer clear of any details, such as bows or draping, that start around the hip line. A bracelet or a bangle would balance the bare arm, but make sure that your earrings blend in well. Silver would be very attractive.

The fabric needs to be rather pliable, like a crêpe or a stretch fabric, but make sure that it is in a fairly heavy weight so that it doesn't cling.

Short-waisted. This style of dress is really not too much of a problem for short-waisted figures, providing you avoid any draping or other detail that starts at waist level. One style you could easily wear is the simple halter-neck dress that is almost tubular in shape. To make this look more stylish and

... fitted, one shoulder top ...

... halter neckline ...

... softer, fuller skirt

... tapers to hemline ...

...wrapover bodice...

...draped from one shoulder...

...waterfall frill from the hip...

...uneven hemline...

flattering, go for a softer, fuller top that tapers down to a narrow hemline. The effect can be stunning, particularly if you keep it simple. Go for very high-heeled shoes or slingbacks, and bracelets and bangles with toning earrings for your jewellery. If you choose to wear bangles, then one on each arm can look very attractive, providing they are not too heavy, particularly if you wear one high up on the arm above the elbow and the other at the wrist. Soft draping fabrics would work well in this style.

Top heavy. Obviously, a one-shoulder style does not suit the bigger-busted figure. It is much better to go for a wrapover shape which is still fairly slim but which doesn't fit too tightly over the bust. This will avoid putting too much emphasis where you don't want it. Keep the top half of the dress very simple, with fitted sleeves that narrow into the wrist. Then, to balance your smaller hip shape, have a soft 'waterfall' frill that falls from the hips to the ankles – a detail that softens an otherwise rather severe look.

Keep jewellery simple. A single pair of beautiful earrings – perhaps glass imitations of rubies or sapphires – can be very striking, especially with black. A not too soft fabric would work well for this style of dress, for example crêpe-de-chine or even velvet.

Hour glass. You always need to emphasise your waistline, but you need to be careful about it. With a straighter-cut dress like this one, simply adding a belt to give it waist definition would look awful – a sack of potatoes tied around the middle. There is nothing wrong with a one-shoulder bodice, providing that you are not too big-busted and that the fabric is one that carefully drapes over the bust rather than pulls. To give your waistline strong definition, you need to lift the front of the skirt around the waistline on one side only, so that the front of the dress is raised and falls into an uneven hem. This gives a waistline detail that is quite unmistakable without being too bold. Again, if you are wearing a one-shoulder dress, the bare arm will look good with a bangle or a bracelet, and matching earrings. Don't wear long chains or strings of beads.

A Basic Evening Wardrobe

If you don't want to lavish an enormous amount of time and money on buying a different outfit for every occasion, or if you are not particularly 'dressy' and feel that the whole business of dressing up can be rather a bore, then evening separates will be more your style. Evening separates are ideal for low budgets because you can wear them in many different ways and make them look different each time. They are clothes that you can 'dress up' or 'dress down' depending on the nature of the occasion. But if they are to look good enough for special evening functions, they do need to be made of rich, rather sumptuous fabrics, and you do need to choose the right accessories.

One of the most versatile of items is a simple velvet skirt – either ankle length or, possibly, even mid-calf. It should be straight cut, maybe with a high centre slit at the back. This shape of skirt looks very good with a taffeta or chiffon blouse tucked in at the waist, and it looks equally attractive with a beaded or sequined round-neck or vest-style top. It is up to you to ring the fashion changes as you want. The possibilities are endless. You could even wear it with a glittery knitted top if the occasion seemed to warrant it.

Alternatively, a fuller, more circular velvet skirt can look equally chic. Wear it with a sumptuous wrapover satin top with batwing sleeves, or with a top with a plunging back. In general, if you are wearing a more fully structured skirt, wear your top or blouse tucked into it to give it the most flattering shape.

Trousers, especially in velvet in a classic cut, or in soft silk jersey in a style that drapes cleverly, can look very glamorous for evening wear. Teamed with a striking top and worn, perhaps, with a satin-look quilted jacket (like a smoking jacket or dinner jacket), they can have a very coordinated look for evening separates. For an out of the ordinary, rather *avant garde* look, try wearing the jacket done up with nothing underneath, and just add a sparkling diamante necklace and a pair of matching drop earrings.

For a more romantic look, and if you want to wear a blouse, choose one with a big lacy collar and tie a ribbon bow at

... wrapover satin top ...

... circular skirt ...

... diamonte jewellery ...

... smoking jacket ...

... sequin vest and velvet skirt .....

... Classic Cut trousers ....

the neck as a special detail. This looks equally good with a skirt or trousers. **Fabrics** are vital in making evening separates work. Just by taking a plain velvet skirt and wearing it with a top or blouse in a much more luxurious fabric like silk, taffeta or satin, you have turned simple separates into a stunning evening outfit. Colours, too, make all the difference. If you want a velvet skirt or pair of trousers that won't date and that you won't tire of wearing too quickly, then stick to black. This is a colour that you can wear with a whole range of other, different, colours. It can look very eye-catching contrasted with pure white or silver, but it will also go well with rich red, purple or bright 'electric' blue. Follow through the colour you choose in your accessories. Colour coordination can make all the difference when you are trying to look stylish and elegant.

Royal accessories

A woman in the Princess of Wales' position has a considerable amount of jewellery in her wardrobe, but the last thing that Diana would do is to overload herself with it. She is a perfect example of the rule that there is no need to over-dress and never any need to wear too much jewellery. She is always tasteful and full of style, whether she is wearing an exquisite diamond necklace or pendant, or a simple strand of beads. Her earrings and bracelets always match or complement each other; her jewellery always tones with the style of dress she is wearing. For shoes, belts and bags, the Princess doesn't vary her style much from her daytime wear. The main difference is in her colour choice. Gold and silver are her prefer-ences, depending on which colour best suits the rest of her outfit. The ensemble is still very neat—low-heeled plain pumps, a small matching clutch-bag and very, rarely, a pair of gloves (she wore them, for example, for the State Opening of Parliament). If her dresses do not have a matching sash or cummerbund, she chooses one in a metallic shade, in silver, which sets off her dress beautifully. The Princess shows how to dress with style by making her accessories enhance, not detract from, the splendour of her dresses.

The Princess's taste in jewellery is simple but effective. Above; she matches her jewellery to her Bellville Sassoon dress at the premiere of For Your Eyes Only; *right; a more formal occasion in Canberra in an evening dress by Murray Arbeid.*

Cover-ups. What to wear on top of your evening gown is a perennial problem. It seems a terrible shame to wear a beautiful evening dress with a heavy tweed coat on top of it. The obvious choice is a shawl or a stole, which is fine if the distance from the car to the front door isn't too great and the weather isn't going to soak you or freeze you on the way. Fur coats or jackets are another possibility although, even if synthetic, a rather costly one. The Princess has occasionally worn a fur jacket, but it is known that she is not happy wearing something that used to belong to a living animal. Her favourite choice is, in fact, a velvet cloak, (see above), and highly suitable it is too. Designed for her during her pregnancy by Gina Fratini, it has since been worn on many occasions. It is ideal because it covers any style of dress and, most important, because it does not crush or crease the superb ballgowns the Princess wears underneath. If you have to attend a lot of formal evening occasions, it is well worth investing in one of these.

Another choice is a satin jacket, often lightly quilted (a look that was very popular a few years ago). These make excellent evening jackets when worn with simpler, rather straighter-cut, dresses or separates; they are not really suitable over ballgowns. Go for a 'big' shape that doesn't fit too snugly, otherwise it will crease everything you have on underneath. If you shop around, they are not too expensive to buy. Choose a colour like black that will coordinate with more or less any other colour you want to wear.

Accessories check-list

If you tend to wear a very simple style of evening dress, you will need to rely on your accessories to make you stand out. Apart from jewellery, the accessories you need for the evenings are very different from those you have in the daytime. Here is a check-list to use as a guide to the accessories you should have for evening wear.

Jewellery. The rules are much the same as ever; don't wear too much and don't mix too many styles together. For instance, pearls and diamante go well together, but diamante earrings combined with gold chains and a pearl bracelet will not look stylish at all. Clever, bold, fakes can look very good; but don't dress up as though you were wearing the Crown Jewels. This is only impressive as an example of bad taste. Try colour matching your dress and your jewellery; if you are in red try rubies in glass or diamante; if in light creams or whites, go for pearls or crystals; and blue is marvellous with sapphires or steel coloured silver.

Belts. A sash, cummerbund or very narrow belt are the only styles worn for the evenings. Pick something in silver, gold, or very soft leather. Sometimes fabric belts in moire or velvet—particularly if they are tastefully trimmed in silver or gold, look extremely good.

Shoes. A plain simple court shoe, in a colour that matches or tones with your outfit, is the best. You should therefore stick to the main evening colours, such as silver, gold and bronze, and black. Don't go for anything too heavy: black suede or patent leather look slightly less heavy than real leather.

If you want to adapt the style of your shoe and at the same time add a bit of extra appeal to your footwear, you can buy a clip-on bow or pom. This can be very effective if you buy one that matches the colour of your dress. If, for example, you are wearing a blue dress with black shoes, then try adding a blue bow to your shoe. Satin court shoes, which often come in white only, are perfect for dyeing to match the colour of your dress. They are fairly inexpensive, so you could almost afford to get a new pair for a special occasion, or to buy several and dye them in a range of different colours.

Slingback shoes (the style that has a shoe front with a strap back) are a good in-between style for those times when a shoe might be too clumsy but a sandal would be too casual. Sandals and mules are fine for some types of evening wear, but are not very stylish for formal occasions. Diana never wears them.

For evenings, you can often allow yourself to go for a higher heel, as long as it suits the dress you are wearing. Looking a little taller does no harm to most evening dresses, particularly if you are a little on the short side. But make sure that they are comfortable and that you can walk and dance in them.

Scarves. These are not, of course, for use around the neck, or in any other place they are usually associated with. A longer scarf is ideal as a cummberbund around the waist, especially with evening separates. You can find some rather luxurious looking scarves in silver or gold thread fabrics, lamé or simply in bright coloured silk or satin. They are a great way to introduce a strong colour into a plain outfit, and they are fairly inexpensive, at least compared to good belts.

Tights. If you are wearing black, then black tights are the answer. Choose finer denier tights (about 10 denier), which don't look so heavy and thick on the leg, and will be much more attractive with lighter, more delicate evening fabrics. Patterned tights work well only if your dress is very simple, or if the pattern links with the fabric of the dress. Fishnets look awful with a silk chiffon ballgown, but fine lacy tights can look great with a lacy dress. A fine silky almost shimmering texture can often look very attractive. Stick to natural colours or to black, as too bright a leg can ruin an otherwise sophisticated evening look.

Bags. The smaller your bag the better. A clutch or tiny pouch is best or, failing that, a very small shoulder bag. Silver, gold or black are the best colours. Velvet or a beaded fabric can also make attractive evening bags.

Ribbons. These can be very useful as an evening accessory. Wear one as a choker around your neck, or use a wider ribbon as a sash around the waist. Be careful to choose colours that match your outfits, and enough to tie it in a bow and have some hanging at the back.

Evening glamour

Diana's approach to glamour is refreshingly different for a member of the Royal Family, with her often quite daring plunge-front dresses, one-shoulder designs and revealing strapless creations. She carries them off with great aplomb, knowing that her young figure is good enough to reveal, her long neck graceful enough to emphasise and her skin is flawless, even in those more difficult areas such as upper arms, back and elbows.

When you wear a revealing outfit, it is essential to check that the body skin is satin smooth, soft and clear. So great attention must be paid to the underarms, which small razors, or depilatory creams, will soon ensure are fuzz-free. The back should be kept clear with a daily bath or shower (preferably with a softening gel or bath additive) and it helps to use a bristle back brush to stimulate the circulation, and a handful of sea salt or exfoliating cream to slough off the dead cells which can give the skin a dull, dingy appearance. Upper arms can let you down if they have 'gooseflesh'. This is sometimes hereditary, but it can also be caused by dietary deficiency. Fish oils or cod liver oil capsules should be included in the diet. And you can take abrasive action on the skin with sea salt mixed to a smooth paste with a little almond oil, rubbed over the roughened area at bathtime. Keep the skin supple, flexible and soft with liberal helpings of body lotion, lighter in summer and richer in winter. Elbows can be softened and whitened by dipping them into a bowl of warmed almond oil with a few drops of lemon juice.

Add extra lustre to your body with a hint of gold sparkle powder or gel. Apply to highlight areas such as shoulders, collar-bone or cleavage. If your bosom is not your greatest asset, then use a dark face shader and a fat blusher brush to 'create' or draw in a well blended cleavage line. Add extra sparkle to your face with a gold-flecked lip colour, or an extra glossy lip shine, as the Princess often does. Use a sparkling eye-shadow or simply highlight the centre of your eyelids with a gold or silver shadow. And whilst you may not be wearing a tiara, you can highlight your hairstyle with diamante combs and slides and other eye-catching hair accessories.

Alternative evening dress

Finally, a few words about alternative ways of expanding your range of evening wear, which are cheaper and often more fun than the conventional ones.

It is almost impossible these days for women to hire evening dresses. But that doesn't make it exclusively a male preserve. The 'tuxedo' look for women is not just accepted but very fashionable. You can hire just the jacket (white is as good as black) and trousers and then add lots of feminine details—a frilly silk or chiffon blouse, very high court shoes, a cummerbund and glamorous accessories. Antique markets or shops are well worth a look. Beautiful bead or sequin dresses and tops from the 1920s and '30s, cut short fur capes and velvet tops, are styles from yester-year that are popular again today. And antique shops can be marvellous places for accessories, particularly jewellery. Old jet, pearls or rhinestones can be exquisite for evening wear. Antique velvet or beaded purses can make lovely little bags for evening. Lastly, 'nearly new' shops are the best of the second hand dress shops. The clothes may be more expensive, but they often include infrequently used dresses from wealthy women and celebrities. It is possible to find truly wonderful dresses in tip-top condition at half their original prices.

CHAPTER FIVE

Weddings

*The bridal procession leaving St Paul's
Cathedral, watched by millions across
the world. The country had seen nothing
to equal this ceremony since the Coronation
nearly thirty years before.*

On Wednesday the 29th of July, 1981, the whole of the United Kingdom of Great Britain and Northern Ireland was on holiday. The previous night, beacons had been lit across the country and over quarter of a million people had thronged the streets of central London to watch one of the most magnificent firework displays in living memory. At 11.15 a.m. next morning, at St Paul's Cathedral, Lady Diana Spencer was married to Prince Charles, the Prince of Wales and the future King of England. The nation gave up the day to celebration. There were parties in the streets, in homes and in gardens. And it was not just one country that rejoiced. The number of people across the world who watched the occasion on television was estimated at a staggering 250 million.

The wedding was the culmination of months of rehearsal and of endless planning that would have done credit to a major military campaign. It was the high point of a romance that had touched the world's heart, and a source of national pride and joy in an uncertain decade in a troubled century.

Most brides have an audience, but few face the daunting prospect of getting married before an audience of hundreds of millions—even if only 2,500 of them were present in the flesh. Marriage, however, even for Kings, Queens and Princes, is a very personal matter; an affirmation of mutual love and respect. Amidst all the pomp and splendour of the occasion, romance was still very much the order of the day, and there was magic in the air.

Foremost in Diana's mind must have been her wedding dress, and the dresses of the bridesmaids. By the time of the wedding, Diana had established her own distinctive style. In keeping with the mood of the moment, it was romantic and feminine. The wedding dress was to carry through this theme. The task of designing it, and the dresses of the bridesmaids, went to a young husband-and-wife design team, David and Elizabeth Emanuel. The couple had already designed several dresses for Diana, including the famous black taffeta ballgown that she wore on her first public engagement. Designing the wedding dress, however was both a much greater privilege and a much greater responsibility, as the Emanuels were aware. Inevitably, there was criticism of the result, but the most important thing was that the bride, and her groom, seemed delighted with it. The new Princess looked every inch a future Queen.

The dress was made of ivory silk taffeta and lace, embroidered with mother-of-pearl sequins and pearls. With it, Diana wore a tiara as a head-dress with a tulle veil, and a train that measured 25 feet in length. Like every bride, Diana respected the ancient traditions of marriage, wearing 'something old and something new, something borrowed and something blue.' The 'old' was the lace, which had once belonged to Queen Mary; the 'new' was the silk; the Spencer family tiara (a family heirloom) and the diamond earrings which belonged to her mother were 'borrowed'; and a tiny bow of 'blue' ribbon was sewn into the waistband of the dress.

The bridesmaids' dresses were all in the same coloured silk and lace trim as the wedding dress, the four younger bridesmaids wearing 'ballerina' length dresses and Lady Sarah Armstrong-Jones wearing a full length dress. Each had a ruffle around the neck, a fitted bodice with sash-tied waist, and a two-tiered skirt with lace trim. The most detailed parts of the dresses were the puffed elbow-length

Facing page; the Prince and Princess of Wales, newly pronounced man and wife, put the seal on their wedding and their romance with a famous kiss, touching the hearts of the vast crowd gathered to cheer them at Buckingham Palace.

sleeves, with a lace and bow detail. The pageboys wore military-style suits, to correspond with Prince Charles's uniform of a Commander of the Royal Navy.

Diana achieved what all brides set out to do—to blend their own dress with their bridesmaids' and pageboys' outfits to create a harmonious overall look. In Diana's case, the whole ensemble was designed to give this effect. For other women, this can be more difficult. The problem is that most women do not know where to start and, without expert advice, they can become worried and confused. The starting point, of course, must be the wedding dress itself. As David Emanuel says 'you need to choose a style that is flattering to you. It is so easy to go out and buy something special that doesn't suit you at all.' Most women have an image of how they want to look at their weddings. Unfortunately, it is not always the right one. The rule is not to be too impulsive. If you feel you need to ask for specialist advice, talk to the assistants in specialist bridal shops or in the better department stores. It is wise to go shopping with a friend or relative whose opinion you trust and who you know understands and sympathises with your style of dress. Their support can give you valuable confidence that what you have chosen is right. Beware, however, of the sort of friend or relative who takes over completely. They may have images of their own which can be far more inappropriate than anything you could dream up for yourself. The final say must be yours if you are to have the confidence you need on the day of your wedding.

Before you go shopping for wedding dresses and bridesmaids' dresses, there are some general guidelines worth bearing in mind. Firstly, look through the magazines, particularly the ones devoted to brides. Styles for wedding dresses change with the times, like fashion in general, and they will tell you what is in and out of vogue. If you have a figure problem—and there are very few women who are model shape and height—then you need to take account of all the points that relate to dressing to suit your shape (see page 112). Wedding dresses are usually white or cream, and light pale colours can highlight some figure faults. Never be afraid to try on lots of different styles of dresses, even if you are sure of the one you want. The more you cast aside, the more confident you will be in your final choice. And you may find, for example, that the 'crinoline' style you fancied doesn't suit you nearly as well as a high neck, slimmer 'Edwardian' style. Work out your budget, and always buy the main items first. It would be silly to spend a lot of money on a fantastic head-dress without knowing how much the dresses for you and the bridesmaids are likely to cost. Finally, don't leave shopping for such important clothes to the last minute. If you are making your own and the bridesmaids' dresses yourself, or having a dressmaker to do it for you, you should work out patterns and fabrics in plenty of time to allow for fittings and final make-up. Even if you are buying everything from shops, it is highly likely that alterations will be required, and such alterations take time.

Planning your wedding outfits not only takes time, it also takes money. For many people, cost is the governing factor. Getting married is never cheap. However, this doesn't mean that working within a smaller budget need make you look less attractive. There are ways of cutting corners without losing style. One good idea is to buy the wedding dress itself from a specialist shop, and then to have the bridesmaids' dresses home-made. The simpler styling of these means that they are easier to make up, and there is less chance of last minute disappointments. If you are planning any form of home dressmaking, be sure that you buy all the fabric you need. There is nothing worse than running out of material half way through the third bridesmaid's dress.

A cheerful wedding group. Diana had five bridesmaids—Lady Sarah Armstrong-Jones, India Hicks, Sarah Jane Gaselee, Catherine Cameron and Clementine Hambro—all dressed in a style to suit Diana's own. The two pageboys, Lord Nicholas Windsor and Edward van Cutsem, were dressed in military style, echoing the Prince's Naval uniform.

Work out a theme for your wedding, both in colour and in style. You might, for example, like to have a dress with a 'period', perhaps Victorian, flavour to it. Diana followed this course, and chose bridesmaids' dresses in complementary style. They also matched in colour. Most brides wear white for formal weddings, but Diana herself chose the palest shade of cream, with ivory. Many fashion experts say that this is a much more flattering colour, particularly for such a special occasion, than white, which can be rather harsh and difficult to wear. If, however, you do want to stick with traditional white for your own dress, there is no reason why you cannot bend the rules a little with the bridesmaids dresses to introduce a bit more colour into the occasion.

The best fabrics for wedding dresses are soft and delicate rather than stiff and harsh. The most suitable are lace, tulle, taffeta, voile, and almost sheer, lightweight, cottons. The more expensive your wedding dress, the finer the fabric will be. And while you may be aiming for a romantic and feminine effect, remember that a few telling details will work far more effectively than frothy, fussy frills, bows, tiers and complicated accessories.

Finally, it is worth giving some thought to the groom's clothes. You may not be directly responsible for these, but you can, and should, have some say in them. In some ways, you husband-to-be is your most important accessory, and there is no reason why he should not dress in a style that harmonises with the other outfits you have planned. In any wedding—not just a Royal one—the bride is the star. Years into the future, she will look into the family photograph album, and see herself as she was then. It is worth going to a lot of trouble to get it right.

Bridesmaids and pageboys

Diana reassures her youngest bridesmaid, Clementine Hambro, with assistance from the Queen. All the bridesmaids carried matching bouquets or posies of flowers.

There are no particular rules on how many bridesmaids and pageboys you should have. You need not have any at all if you don't want them. Most brides tend to have between two and four, but it is really the number of eligible relatives and friends that is most likely to determine how many you have. Pageboys tend to be young boys, generally under ten years old. Bridesmaids, however, can be almost any age. Some brides have all their bridesmaids roughly the same age, and others have a mixture of ages. You need to discuss your plans with prospective bridesmaids (or their mothers) well in advance. In particular, you need to settle the questions of who is paying for what. Are you footing the bill for dress, head-dress, flowers and shoes, or are you only bearing part of the cost? If these matters are not settled beforehand, they can lead to disagreements and ill-feeling.

If you have some sort of 'theme' for your wedding, you will want the bridesmaids to follow through in the same sort of style. If, however, you have bridesmaids of widely different ages, you need to be careful that the style of bridesmaid's dress you choose doesn't make either age group look silly. The same sort of considerations apply to colour. Don't force one bridesmaid into a colour that doesn't suit her simply because another one looks very pretty in it.

For spring and summer weddings, pastel colours in a plain or printed fabric can look very fresh and attractive for bridesmaids' dresses. Of course, no bride wants to be overshadowed by her bridesmaids, so patterns that are too bold and colours that are too strong are not a good idea. Instead of dressing all the bridesmaids in a single colour like pink, or in a selection of different colours such as pink, pistachio and pale blue, why not stick to one colour but in different shades? For example, your oldest bridesmaid could be in dark blue, the youngest in a delicate shade of pale blue, and your own dress in white. The bouquets could follow the same colour theme of blue and white, the bridesmaids' in one style and the bride's in another. For a powerful colour theme for a winter wedding, the bride could be in snowy white, with the bridesmaids in a stronger, darker colour—Royal blue in velvet would look very striking. Colour coordination of this sort can look extremely attractive when it is properly done, and can add a great deal to the pleasure of the occasion.

Most specialist wedding shops will be able to supply you with, and advise you on, the right bridesmaids' dresses to complement your own looks. So too will most large department stores with a wedding department. You may find, however, that you have a much wider choice of colour fabric and style if you have the bridesmaids dresses made by a dressmaker, and often it is cheaper too.

Bear in mind that younger girls like to wear their bridesmaids dresses as party dresses. It is worth keeping an eye open for special details. If the dress is ankle length with a low frill, for example, this could perhaps be removed later to turn it into a shorter length dress that would be ideal for a special party.

Little boys hate being made to look or feel silly. It will only cause problems on the day if you have a pageboy who is deep red with embarrassment and only wants to keep out of sight. Generally, they are happy to wear the traditional velvet pageboy suit, or you can go for a more military uniform style or, for slightly older boys, you can hire a formal dinner suit (not top hat and tails, more an evening dress suit). If you want to buy, most large department stores stock a small range of pageboy outfits. And the velvet waistcoat, trousers, shirt and bow tie ensemble is something that boys can wear again.

Wedding accessories

For the Royal wedding, as much care would have gone into the choice of accessories as into everything else. Diana followed her almost invariable rule of keeping her accessories simple. The only jewellery she wore was the simple pair of earrings she borrowed from her mother. Her shoes or rather wedding slippers, on the other hand were a little more elaborate than usual; the only similarity between them and her everyday style was the choice of a low heel. Created by Clive Shilton, they were made of ivory silk, top stitched and decorated with mother-of-pearl sequins, giving them a rather 'regency' look which suited both the dress and the occasion perfectly. As a head-dress, Diana wore a tiara, with a wide tulle veil, and a 25-foot long train. Individually, each of her accessories was thus fairly distinctive, and Diana sensibly kept them to a minimum.

The veil and head-dress. These are probably the most important accessories in the bride's outfit. The style you choose will depend on the style of the wedding dress, and on your hairstyle—obviously, if you have short hair then scattering silk flowers through it would look silly. There is a wide variety of head-dresses to choose from. There are head-bands of flowers (usually silk or dried) that are traditionally worn on the back of the head; there are tiny juliet caps, again worn towards the back of the head; and there are garlands of pearls or flowers (try a ring of fresh or silk flowers to match your bouquet), which sit on the top of your head. A ribbon tied as a band around the head can look very effective; and ribbons or braid can be twisted and plaited to make a very pretty head-band. This works very well with long hair, especially when the hairstyle is simple. One or two flowers and pearl hair combs would be all the additions you would need. A large-brimmed hat can also look very effective, but only if it suits the style of your dress and is made in a very lightweight fabric.

A fine veil falling over the face can look extremely pretty. Be careful to choose one that fixes easily to your head-dress. Length is very much a matter of personal choice, but do keep in mind your shape and height when choosing a veil. A rather wide, stiff short veil can be unflattering to shorter or plumper figures. And if you have pearl or a flower trim in your dress, choose a veil that blends in with this detail. It would be sensible to take your head-dress and veil to your hairdresser several weeks before the wedding so that either they or your hairstyle can be altered if need be.

Underskirts. With certain styles of wedding dress, an underskirt is vital. You may simply need an extra layer to flounce out your skirt or, if you have a full, circular crinoline-style of skirt, you may well need a hooped underskirt.

Jewellery. Despite the grandness of the occasion, you need to keep your jewellery quiet and unobtrusive. Simple stud earrings, tiny drops, a strand of pearls or a fine chain are some of the more suitable choices.

Shoes. These must, above all, be comfortable. Unless you are wearing a shorter dress, they will hardly even be noticed. A simple white court shoe in leather, or a fabric such as satin, is ideal. Sandals tend to look a little messy. Keep the heel height to one that you can walk easily in. If your dress requires you to wear slightly higher heels than you are used to, it is a good idea to wear the shoes indoors a few times before the wedding to get used to them.

Bouquets. Flowers or bouquets are also important accessories. There is a wide range of styles available although, if you opt for fresh flowers, you might find your choice limited by what is available at the season. Some brides carry a single stem flower, such as a rose, rather than a bouquet. Don't forget to colour coordinate your flowers with your dress and with the bridesmaids and their accessories.

Special accessories. Some specialist accessories are made to team with a wedding dress; for example, a lacy parasol (the Princess herself had one made for the wedding) or fine-mesh or lacy gloves in long, short or even fingerless styles. These can all look very attractive when properly used, but don't clutter yourself up.

Bridesmaids' accessories. These should be pretty but not too flamboyant, and they should complement the style of the dress. Diana's bridesmaids each had fresh flower garlands in their hair, except for Lady Sarah Armstrong-Jones who had flower hair combs as a head-dress. All carried matching flowers in a tiny basket or in a posy.

The most important thing about bridesmaids' accessories is that they should be fairly uniform. For a head-dress, a simple garland, hair combs or a headband (rather like an Alice band) is ideal and will suit most hairstyles. Bouquets and posies should always be kept fairly small, whatever the age or size of your bridesmaid. They, too, could either match the colour of the dress, or tone in with it. Small, delicate flowers are much better than large, flamboyant ones. Fresh flowers are probably nicest, but silk or dried flowers will do perfectly well, and will be more resilient in small and nervous hands.

Keep all other accessories to a minimum. Fine lacy gloves, possibly in a fingerless style, often go well with bridesmaids' outfits, and the younger ones love wearing them. The choice of shoes depends on how much money you have got to spend. A good idea is to choose plain pumps for grown-up bridesmaids or simple slip-ons for the younger ones, and then use a special shoe dye to match them to the dresses. Fabric shoes will dye particularly well.

Going away. Almost the only thing that survives of what was once an elaborate bridal trousseau is the 'going away' outfit. The Princess herself changed after the wedding into a suit—a pastel peach skirt, bolero style jacket, and toning cream blouse, topped with a matching tricorn-shaped hat. Like all other brides, she chose something that she could wear again. Your own choice will probably depend on where you are going. Generally you will need something that will be comfortable to travel in (see page 57) but if you are leaving the reception to go on to a hotel, or even a dinner party, a smart silk dress or suit would be more appropriate. Whatever you choose, it should be simple and comfortable. After wearing a wedding dress for a few hours, you need something you can relax in.

A dress for your shape

Wedding dresses, although they are said to make every woman look magical, can, in fact, be very unflattering. Their voluminous cut and the white or ivory colours in which they are usually made, can highlight any faults in your figure unless you are very careful about the style you choose. Here are some suggestions.

Pear shaped. You need to transfer the emphasis away from the hips and onto the upper part of the body. The pretty ivory silk wedding dress, with matching heavy lace trim, shown here, is similar in mood to the one worn by the Princess. The lower v-neck trimmed with deep heavy lace, and the full elbow length sleeves with matching lace trim, ensure plenty of detail on the fitted bodice without making it too fussy. Follow the detail through on the skirt, but at the hem rather than on the hips.

Short-waisted. Steer clear of deep sash wasitlines or a too fitted bodice. A drop-waist dress with a 1920s feel to it would be ideal, and you could follow through the period look with your accessories. Wear a garland low on the forehead, or just a ribbon tied as a headband. A soft flocked simple fabric would be in keeping with the style.

Hourglass. A fairly shaped, almost fitted, dress will flatter your figure. The style shown here has a narrow high-neck collar, pin-tucked fitted bodice, full sleeves that taper into the wrist, and a full circular skirt. A deep sash belt is worn at the waist. Keep the fabric plain, with just a narrow frill trim around the neck and cuffs. Very fine white cotton lace trim would be ideal.

Top heavy. High necklines, pin-tucks and narrow frills are not right for this shape. However, you don't have to avoid all detail on the upper part of the body. A slightly scooped neckline with a very deep frill—almost a separate tier—which can be worn off the shoulder, can look very good. You need to show off a waistline, as otherwise you disappear into a froth of white lace. The sleeves should be narrow; in summer this style could even be worn sleeveless.

..dried flowers..

heavy lace trim

bouquet of dried flowers....

single flower...

drop waist

hemline detail

...fitted bodice...

...lace trim

...deep frill....

...bouquet of one coloured flowers...

posy

...antique-look lace...

The finishing touches

Your hair and make up are the final, essential details. They provide the finishing touches to the way you will look on your wedding day, and they can be crucial to your happiness and self-confidence.

There is one thing on which all the leading hairdressers and beauty consultants are agreed: don't make any drastic changes to your looks on your wedding day. A completely untested new hair style, or a new range of colours in your make-up, can prove very unnerving. You are likely to be quite nervous enough as it is without adding to the problem. If you are thinking of altering your normal hairstyle, then talk to your hairdresser about it and have a practice run a few weeks beforehand. You are better off anyway with an easy and simple style. Remember that you may well want it to last, looking clean and shiny, throughout the day.

Diana's make up on the wedding day was in the hands of top make-up artist Barbara Daly, who has worked closely with the Princess. She has some sound words of advice about how to apply your make-up so that you look calm, cool and collected and, of course, beautiful on your wedding day.

Firstly, don't wear anything on your face that you are not sure of. You want to be yourself, not some painted face that no one will recognise. If in doubt, leave it off. On the other hand, going without make-up at all is almost as bad. Whites and creams can have a very draining effect on the complexion, and you will probably look a little pale anyway because of the stress that the ceremony brings. Often a little more eye make-up than usual, using a natural shade like grey or brown, can be most effective and will give your eyes the depth they need. Carefully outlining the eyes with kohl can also give them a definite and positive shape, helping to counteract the influence of so much white. Always experiment before the day.

Choose a fairly pale foundation, matched carefully to your complexion. This will give your face a good overall base colour, which will last you a few hours. Plenty of face powder, to stop shine, is essential. You tend to perspire more when you are tense, and this includes the face.

When it comes to lipstick, Barbara Daly has a useful tip. Use a strong lipstick, and apply it thickly. Then blot it and gently rub it in with a tissue. This removes some of the excess colour, but at the same time, it fixes it more firmly in place. It will stay on longer, and will stand up to all the kissing you may find yourself doing.

Stick to your favourite perfume, but don't shower yourself with too much of it as perfume can be very pungent.

Finally, don't decide at the last moment that your face needs the full works and set off for saunas, face packs and all the rest. The most immediate effect of all these is to encourage spots and blemishes to show up, which is the last thing you want to happen on your wedding day.

If you bear these points in mind and carefully test the make-up you will be wearing during the preceding weeks, and if you know that you are wearing a dress that suits you, you will know when the time comes that you are looking your best. You will not have to worry about your appearance and you will be able to concentrate on the events of the day. You will have gone a long way towards ensuring that your wedding will be a day to remember for the rest of your life.

CHAPTER SIX

Maternity Wear

Throughout her pregnancy, the Princess looked radient, young and fashionable. Here she wears one of her 'fun' picture sweaters—a distinctive 'Australian' design by Jenny Kee featuring a Koala bear. It was typical of Diana's fresh and stylish approach to maternity wear.

Above; the proud parents leave St Mary's hospital, Paddington, on 22nd June 1982 with their son, Prince William of Wales. Diana wears a comfortable loose-fitting dress with a favourite collar style. Facing page; the Princess, by now well into pregnancy, relaxes at a polo match. She had several of these soft, simple smocks, designed in the style of the Chelsea Design Company.

Motherhood was a turning point in Princess Diana's life. Since the birth of her child, she has found a new maturity and new stylishness; and she has managed to combine the exacting roles of wife, Princess, and loving mother to Prince William, with great success. Family life is clearly a matter of enormous importance to both her and Prince Charles. Certainly, on the day she emerged from St Mary's Hospital in Paddington, with her newborn son, whe was a picture of radiant happiness.

Radiant happiness was, indeed, the keynote of Diana's appearance throughout her pregnancy. She made no attempt to keep out of the public eye. On the contrary, she seemed determined to project her own happiness and satisfaction at carrying an unborn baby. From the start, it was clear that she was not going to allow pregnancy to affect her sense of style. Her clothes were never frumpy or boring. There were none of those billowing maternity smocks that tend to make women look fat rather than pregnant. Instead, she chose unfussy clothes in beautiful simple styles and fabrics, in soft delicate colours for daytime and deeper, richer colours for evening wear. Her dresses and coats, incorporating many of the 'Diana' details, made her look very feminine and very appealing. They aroused the admiration of many other women, pregnant or not, and showed the manufacturers of maternity wear to be in need of a shake-up. Here, as elsewhere, she set an example that was fun to follow.

Summer pregnancies, especially if you are in the later months, can make you feel very uncomfortable. However, as Diana has shown, it is still possible to look pretty and stylish. Note her use of colour: for maternity wear, she chose soft 'ice-cream' colours which not only make you look cool, but make you feel cool as well—light colours reflect the sun whereas dark ones absorb it and the heat it brings. Her clothes were never too tight or restricting. Tight clothes can make you look and feel dreadful. Diana's styles were easy and not restricted by any fussy detail. Her choice of fabrics, of course, was all important. Silk and cotton are always the best choice because they are so cool to wear. Accessories too are important. Luckily, the Princess's preference for low-heeled pumps and flat shoes is ideally suited to the circumstances. In the later stages of pregnancy, tights can be uncomfortable. Diana solved the problem by going bare-legged or by wearing 'pop' socks—knee high socks which, providing you keep the tops hidden (not always possible, even for a Princess), look exactly like tights.

The Princess decided early on that comfort must be the main governing factor in her choice of clothes. Any woman who has been pregnant would agree with that. Also, like most women, she obviously decided that she did not want to have too many specialised maternity outfits. To begin with, her clothes were not very different from her pre-pregnancy outfits. She was, for example, to be seen watching a polo match in the colourful 'Australia' jumper that she had worn before. Colourful knitwear and red cord pants certainly made a very fashionable outfit for a thoroughly modern Princess. Later, when her pregnancy became more obvious, she came to rely more on a few firm favourites, particularly pretty smocks, which she must have felt good in. Of course, because of her public duties and engagements, the Princess has to have a reasonable selection of clothes, but, towards the end of her pregnancy, she had narrowed her choice down to one or two particularly suitable looks. This is a good principle to follow. If you have found a look that suits you and makes you feel good, it is often worth buying two or three outfits in a similar style. Diana demonstrated how well this can work. Two of her particular favourites were dresses in identical styles. Made in very

Above; soft, pretty pastels were a popular choice for Diana's maternity wear. This pretty blue and white spot dress was designed by the Chelsea Design Company. Above right; dressing in a single 'ice-cream' colour throughout makes a very cool and flattering summer outfit—it doesn't emphasise any one part of the body. Diana dressed entirely in pink for Ascot in 1982.

practical lightweight silk, in the style of the Chelsea Design Company, they differed only in the colourway and the pattern of the fabric; one in a green and white spot, the other in fine blue with a white check. The contrasting collar and tie makes a very flattering neckline for a pregnant shape, and provides all the detail that this simple style requires. Another of the Princess's favourites was very similar in style. Again in the style of the Chelsea Design Company, it was in blue with a tiny white spot pattern in a style that was missing the usual smock detail of a high yoke. Instead, a soft frill lies midway between the neck and the bustline and gently falls over the bust into a full smock dress. This style is particularly slimming over the bustline, which is normally enlarged during pregnancy and shouldn't therefore be emphasised in any way.

One image sums up the Princess's approach to pregnancy: Diana wearing a soft powder pink cotton dress that resembles a large overgrown shirt, casual but with no nonsense about it. Her sleeves are rolled back, she is not wearing tights and she has flat shoes on her feet (a style she first wore on her honeymoon). The look is relaxed and informal. A very similar outfit, worn slightly more formally, becomes completely appropriate, even for a relatively smart occasion like Ascot. You don't leave your fashion sense behind when you are pregnant; you use it to enhance the pleasure of one of the happiest times of your life.

Evening clothes can be every bit as glamorous when you are pregnant as when you are not. Diana, throughout her pregnancy, remained as much the fairy tale

Above; a large, simple, overgrown shirt-dress is all that you need to look attractive in pregnancy; Diana in informal mood at a polo match. Right; Diana's evening wear was just as glamorous during pregnancy as it had been before. At the opening of the Barbican Arts Centre in March 1982, she wore this rich red taffeta ballgown designed by Belville Sassoon.

Princess as ever. She stayed faithful to the magical ballgowns that her audience had come to expect of her. If anything, she took advantage of the alterations to her shape that pregnancy brought about, rather than trying to hide them. Two of her full length evening gowns show this particularly well; one in rich red taffeta, worn to London's Barbican centre; the other a luxurious sapphire blue velvet dress which she wore to a charity concert at the Royal Festival Hall at the end of 1981. Both of these were designed by Belville Sassoon. 'The richness of the fabrics makes the dress speak for itself', in the opinion of both David Sassoon and Belinda Belville. There is no need for an overcomplicated design. Certainly, it is hard to see how either of these two gowns could be made more appealing. The blue velvet dress shows how Diana kept her fondness for feminine collar detail during her pregnancy. It has a heavy lace neckline which is slightly lower cut than her more normal daytime high-neck 'pie-frill' blouses. Both this and the red taffeta gown, with its rather more subdued neckline detail, are actually quite 'daring' and make the most of the Princess's altered figure. This sort of neckline works extremely well for evening wear since it immediately takes the

Above; velvet and lace for this simple long evening dress, designed by Belville Sassoon, which the Princess wore to a charity concert at London's Festival Hall in December 1981. Above right; A mid-calf length evening dress can look very glamorous, as Diana demonstrated in this dark blue velvet dress with a large puritan white collar and lace petticoat, all designed by Gina Fratini, at the 25th London Film Festival. Facing page; Diana wears a brightly coloured turquoise coat and hat for the Christmas Day family service at St George's Chapel, Windsor.

eye away from the bulge at the tummy. Both of these dresses demand simple accessories, especially jewellery. A simple string of pearls or precious stones with matching earrings is all that is needed. With the velvet dress, the Princess chose the sapphire and gold pendant necklace that was part of the three-quarter million pound wedding gift from the Saudi Arabian Royal Family. The red taffeta dress, rather more reminiscent of rubies than of sapphires, also has a fairly low-cut neckline, although the only point of style that connects the two dresses is the high waistline. In this case, the dress is not quite so heavily embellished and has a square neckline with narrow lace trim and elbow length sleeves that fan out to reveal the lace trim repeated again at the wrist. A bow trim appears at the centre of the neckline and again on the high waistline. Because this dress does not have such powerful detail as the velvet one, the Princess chose diamond jewellery, giving her a touch of extra sparkle.

Evening maternity clothes need not necessarily be full length. You may feel that a shorter length would be appropriate on some occasions. The Princess wore a simple navy blue velvet dress that was mid-calf length for a visit to the National Film Theatre in November 1981. Designed by Gina Fratini, this dramatic dress was softened by a large lace puritan-style collar, with matching lace trim around the hem. A dress in this style would do for many different occasions, from a cocktail party to dinner at a restaurant or an evening at the theatre.

Above; a coat that incorporates the characteristic 'Diana' neck frill details. Designed by Belville Sassoon, it was worn for the opening of a Chinese Community Centre in Liverpool in April 1982. Above right; a rather similar style for this large-collared coat which the Princess wore to visit a youth centre in Huddersfield in March 1982.

Coats can be a problem during pregnancy. Some women ignore it and simply wear their normal coats undone. This, however, is hardly elegant. It would not be a good example for the Princess of Wales to follow; and of course she didn't. Instead, Diana wore a number of different coats, all extremely stylish and all very positive in design. Many of them, including the colourful tweed coat that the Princess wore on the day that her pregnancy was officially announced (see page 14) were designed by Belville Sassoon, a design team not normally associated with such specialised clothes. In fact, David Sassoon and Belinda Belville designed many of the Princess's maternity clothes. In all of them, there is a simple guiding principle. As David Sassoon explains, 'I felt the need for plenty of collar emphasis and more detail on the upper part of the body to take away immediate eye contact with the tummy bulge.' Diana's coats show how effectively this intention was carried out. For a visit to Leeds, for example, she wore a simple high-neck green velour coat with velvet trim. The velvet front appliqué is an ingenious form of 'detailing' which instantly achieves its desired effect.

In March 1981, six months pregnant, the Princess wore a deep pink mohair coat, which was very simple in style and in what is obviously one of her favourite

The Princess visited Leeds in March 1982 wearing a simple green high-necked coat with a distinctive appliqué detail on the front. The coat was designed by Belville Sassoon, the matching hat by John Boyd.

colours. The large cape collar, with a narrow fringe trim is the only distinctive detail and provides the focal point of the coat. Diana wore another striking coat on her first Christmas day as Princess of Wales, when she joined the rest of the Royal Family for the service at St George's Chapel at Windsor. Her brightly coloured turquoise coat with floral motif trim added a welcome touch of cheerful colour on a cold winter's day.

It is even possible for a coat to incorporate all the characteristic 'Diana' neck frill details that are usually to be seen on her dresses and blouses. The bright deep pink coat that she wore to open a Chinese Community Centre in Liverpool in April 1982 has a square shouldered look with a square-shaped yoke and frill trim. It incorporates all the points that David Sassoon had in mind when designing maternity wear for the Princess.

The Princess pregnant in winter was thus as enterprising and interesting in her choice of clothes as she has been in the summer. It is perhaps fortunate for those who watch Diana's style of dressing so closely that the heir to the throne was born when he was. Had he arrived earlier or later, we would not have seen the Princess in such a wide range of styles.

A maternity wardrobe

For modern women, pregnancy is a much more public affair than it was for their mothers. It is not uncommon for them to work right up to the moment of birth, and most women lead full and active lives throughout their pregnancy. A few specialised maternity outfits are therefore essential. These don't have to cost a fortune. By careful planning and the clever use of a few basic garments, you can look stylish and elegant for a surprisingly small outlay. The first thing to remember is that you will be pregnant for more than one season. Before you buy anything, consider whether you are going to be at your most pregnant during the hottest or coldest months, and plan your clothes accordingly. Your lifestyle—whether you are working or staying at home—will also affect your choice of suitable maternity clothes. However, the outfits suggested here will give you sufficient flexibility to create a variety of looks for more or less any occasion.

You will need a fairly smart dress made from good quality fabric, in a plain colour or a delicate print. Bold prints and patterns are not particularly flattering during pregnancy, particularly as you become bigger. A smart dress will suit you well for an evening occasion and for any special daytime event. Don't go for anything too fussy in style; if you are going to wear this dress a lot, you will soon get tired of too many frills. It is worth looking around your normal clothes shops at this time, especially if the fashion trend is towards softer, bigger-cut dresses. Do remember, however, that not every wider-cut dress or smock will be suitable, particularly if it was not designed for maternity wear.

Separates, especially trousers and tops can be very comfortable. Skirts are somehow never quite as comfortable to wear, or as flattering, as trousers. A drawstring or elasticated waist may suit you, but be careful that it doesn't become too tight. Dungarees and jogging suits have become fashionable maternity clothes and indeed, on the right woman, worn in the right way, they can look marvellous. Be careful, however: it is not only the tummy that expands during pregnancy and if, like

... shirt-style dress ...

... t-shirt ...

... "fun" dungarees ...

blouse....

elegant, simple dress....

bright accessories....

low-heeled shoes....

quite a few women, you become noticeably 'broader in the beam', you will find some of these casual clothes rather unflattering.

Avoid having too many fussy layers—now is not the time to go 'ethnic' in your looks—but coats and jackets are problems that need to be overcome. A simple full coat would be the best style to see you through your pregnancy; be wary of fluffy or hairy fabrics since these can make you look fatter. A soft sporty jacket, say in a simple blouson shape, would be comfortable to wear.

Separates and dresses are most suitable for everyday wear. A simple dress that is easy to wash and that can be worn often is ideal. So is a plain pinafore dress, which can be dressed up or down depending on the circumstances. For instance, a simple pinafore looks good with a t-shirt or a plain blouse, but it can also be given a more feminine, rather dressy, look by wearing it with a lace collar blouse. By combining it with different tops in different colours, you can create a variety of different looks.

Your shape obviously alters constantly throughout pregnancy and you must always remember that you will soon want to get back to your normal figure. The Princess of Wales has in fact become slimmer since the birth of Prince William. But to help your body regain its shape, you must be careful over your choice of maternity underwear. A good supportive bra, not only during pregnancy but also in the early months after your baby is born (especially if you are breast feeding), is essential. Cotton is much pleasanter than nylon and will not make you so hot. Supportive panties may also be necessary, particularly if the pelvic floor muscles begin to sag or ache. These are not perhaps the most elegant of underwear looks, but they are certainly the most practical, and fashion is not your highest priority in circumstances like these.

Footwear becomes particularly important during pregnancy because your feet tend to swell as you put on weight. Go for sensible, but not clumsy, pumps, rather like the ones the Princess often wears. During her pregnancy, she often wore this type of shoe with a small bow detail. High heels, strappy sandals and tight-fitting high boots are all styles that could prove very unfomfortable.

Epilogue

This book has no proper ending. For the Princess of Wales, the last three years have been just a beginning; the first few pages in a story that will continue for many, many years. Admittedly, it has been a spectacular beginning, but all the best stories begin that way. The princess has held our attention from the start and there is no reason why she should not carry on doing so for long into the future.

The Princess's impact is hard to appreciate. If the British Royal Family was popular before, it has now become the focus of avid interest the world over. Diana's flair, and her elegant but modern style, have captivated people throughout the world. It is not just because of her clothes. Diana's warmth of personality and her genuine interest in people have made her the subject of enormous admiration and affection. Her approach to her public duties has been refreshing. She has never adopted strict formality—all too often a disguise for natural shyness or nervousness. We have seen her on walkabouts stopping to shake hands with the old and the handicapped, as well as over-excited children. No one is intentionally ignored.

Children in particular always receive special attention. And in return for her obvious affection, they all adore her. This, and her early days working in a kindergarten, mean that her new role as mother to Prince William comes entirely naturally to her. Family life is obviously going to play a major part in the lives of both her and her husband. A secure and happy Royal Family will be an important national symbol in the years to come.

Diana's style is all of a piece. It shows not just in her clothes, but in her personality as a whole. Like all stylish dressers, she uses her clothes to project her personality and the admiration they have aroused is thoroughly deserved. Fashions, of course, change, but a sense of style does not. The fashions of the late 20th and the early 21st centuries can't be guessed at. But however outlandish they might look if we were to see them now, we can confidently expect the Princess—and, in time, the Queen of England—to interpret them and to incorporate them into her wardrobe with the same good sense and stylishness as she has shown with fashion today. Diana has great individuality, and a mind of her own. We are fortunate to have someone like her as the future Queen of England.

Three wholehearted cheers for the Princess of Wales!

Acknowledgements All photographs by Tim Graham except: page 37, Jim Bennett, Camera Press; pages 109, 110, Patrick Lichfield, Camera Press. Fabric photographs, Angelo Hornak.

Original designer's sketches were provided by the following: page 43, Arabella Pollen; page 46, Warm and Wonderful; page 53, Benny Ong; page 70, Donald Campbell; page 71, Jan Vanvelden; page 78, David Neil; page 92, Gina Fratini; page 93, Belville·Sassoon; page 94, Bruce Oldfield; page 95, Victor Edelstein. Permission for their use is gratefully acknowledged. All other artwork, Lesley Dilcock.

Advice and assistance were given by John Boyd and Barbara Daly. Assistance is also acknowledged from; Chelsea Design Company, Jasper Conran, Caroline Charles, Murray Arbeid, David and Elizabeth Emanuel.